About the Book

The name Cochise struck terror in the hearts of westward moving settlers in the middle 1800's, but the feared and hated Apache chief had genuinely tried to live in peace with the white traders and soldiers who came into Chiricahua territory. This carefully researched biography of Cohise is a moving story of conflict and tragedy, of bravery and betrayal. It points up the dilemma of a sensitive, intelligent Indian leader who had been trained from his boyhood in war and tribal tradition, but who understood the need to accept change.

Abundantly illustrated with drawings that carefully reflect Apache characteristics.

COCHISE

Chief of the Chiricahaus

BY VADA F. CARLSON

Illustrated by William A. Orr

Harvey House, Inc., Publishers
Irvington-on-Hudson, New York

Library of Congress Catalog Card Number 71-148107
Manufactured in the United States of America
ISBN 0-8178-4951-3, Trade Edition. ISBN 0-8178-4952-1, Library Edition

Harvey House, Inc., *Publishers*
Irvington, New York 10533

Contents

1

The Raiders Return

In a cleared section of the lofty mountain valley that was their traditional homesite, a group of Chiricahua Apache youths were engrossed in the competition of a spirited hoop-and-pole game.

The day was mild. Gentle spring breezes drifted down from the jagged sentinel peaks that surrounded the valley, making it a natural fortress. From the grass wickiups of the encampment nearby came sounds of little children playing. Girls and women chattered as they wove useful wicker baskets, tanned deerskins, beaded headbands, braided horsehair bridles for their ponies, and engaged in other woman's work. But the boys at play were too intent on the game to give them any attention. All eyes were upon the tall lad, named Cochise.

In one brown hand he held a slender pole stripped of its bark and painted white; in the other he held loosely a leather-bound grass hoop which he was about to roll along the grass-strewn playing line. Twice he swung it, sighting along the course, then he crouched and rolled it on its way. As it left his fingers, he sent the white pole slithering along the ground after it.

In the moment of suspense that followed there was no sound from the players, but as the hoop wobbled, dipped from side to side, and fell onto the pole, as the tall lad had intended, the spell was broken.

"Cochise! . . . Cochise!" yelled those on his side, while his opponents groaned.

On a deerskin near the gaming area sat the winner's two younger brothers, Juan and Naretena. Juan, the plump, older one, nudged thin and sickly Naretena.

"If you were a good scorekeeper," he scolded, "you'd give our brother another marker. You do want him to win, don't you?"

Naretena's black eyes reproached Juan as he fumbled for a white twig to lay beside the row of markers that were evidence of his brother's prowess in the game.

"I was going to," he mumbled, the flush on his young cheeks deepening. "Of course I want him to win, and you know that very well."

The game continued, with the other side trying hard to match the score of Cochise, but failing.

Again the hoop was handed to Cochise. He took it, poised to throw it, then suddenly froze in mid-action, his head turned slightly to one side. No one was talking, yet a Voice had spoken to him. It had come clearly from somewhere inside his head, and it had distinctly said, "They are coming."

As he hesitated, straightening, the burly youngster who headed the other team laughed tauntingly.

"Ha! The great Cochise is afraid of losing this time. . . . Come on, Cochise. Throw the hoop, or lose points for holding."

Cochise gave no sign of having heard the

words. Instead, he tossed the hoop to Juan and said, "Take my place."

Before Juan, taken off guard, could jump up and take the proper station, Cochise had dropped the white pole and had set off at a run, headed for a steep trail that led from the valley floor to a lookout point on one of the peaks above.

He ran with the greatest ease, bounding like a young deer and seeming almost to float through the clean, sweet air, so firm and sure were his strides. His coppery skin gleamed in the sunlight; his muscles were smooth and firm; his head was held high, a red headband confining his straight black hair. About his middle he wore a breechcloth of pale-figured calico, and on his feet were moccasins of tanned deerskin, high-topped to protect his legs from the thorny brush and needle-sharp cactus that crowded into the narrow trail on the mountainside.

He had gone only a little distance when he heard a sound that brought him to an annoyed halt. Someone was following him up the trail — someone who coughed. That, he knew, would be his little brother, Naretena.

When the boy came into view, running, panting, coughing, Cochise said, half-pityingly, half-reproachfully, "Little Brother! When will you learn not to tag along after me everywhere? The red of fever burns in your face again today. You should be in the wickiup, resting. Go back."

"No." Naretena gasped. "Truly I want to go with you. Please don't make me go back. I want to see them, too."

"You want to see them? How did you know anything about them?" Cochise tried to look stern, but in spite of himself his expression softened. He could never be very harsh with the youngster who so evidently adored him.

"When you hurried away like that," Naretena said, "I knew. They are coming, aren't they? That's why you dropped everything and ran, isn't it?"

Cochise looked hard at the boy's face, wondering how the words he had heard inwardly had been transferred to his brother. He wondered whether that was how it happened that Naretena followed.

"Yes. At least, I think they're coming. I thought I heard a Voice inside my head saying so. Perhaps I did hear a Voice, or it could be that the bottoms of my feet feel the thud of the horses' hoofs on the desert floor down below; I don't know. Maybe my ears are so keen that they pick up sounds from a distance. Anyhow, it suddenly seemed that I should go to the lookout and see for myself whether our father and his warriors were on the way home. . . .Will you go back now?"

Tears glistened in Naretena's eyes. He hung his head, but did not turn back.

"I will come slowly," he murmured.

Cochise sighed. He bent over and placed both his hands on his knees.

"All right. If you must come, I'll carry you. Get on my back."

There was very little flesh on Naretena's young bones. But as the trail became progressively steeper and more rocky, Cochise was glad to reach the lookout and to deposit the boy on a jutting rock.

Aware that danger could be lurking nearby, for the mountains harbored many wild animals, including mountain lions, Cochise cautiously reconnoitered before he showed himself in the more exposed outcrop of rocks. His first glance down into the desert was reassuring. Below, and far into the distance, the desert stretched away, ablaze with the sudden beauty of springtime. Vying with the varied yellows and golds of millions of tiny plants, intent on blooming and seed-producing before the coming summer heat sapped their fertility and dried up their fragile beauty, were patches of pink and red verbena. Paloverde trees bloomed in the washes like puffs of yellow cotton, and cactus flowers made spots of more vivid hues amid deeper greens.

On the flanks of the sentinel peaks saguaros were putting on their white and gold crowns of flowers; cholla wands were tipped with the red flames of their blossoms, and among the gypsy colors of the cactus blooms tall spikes of blue larkspur were cool accents.

"Naretena, come look at this land of ours," Cochise called softly. "How beautiful it is. No wonder our father is determined to keep it safe for us and for our sons-to-be."

Naretena came and stood beside him, his skinny little body naked except for his breechcloth.

"But there's so much of it," he sighed. "It goes on and on and on. Do we need so much? Is there not enough for many others, as well?"

"There should be room enough for many, but our father says we must not allow other people to come here and make homes. He says they would then try to push us out completely. Besides, remember the Mexicans to the south? They have been steadily pushing into our land for many harvest times. That is why we raid them and take their goods. We want them to go back where they belong — to their own people."

"Our mother says they are killing our deer so fast that soon there will be no deer left for us to eat," Naretena said.

"Our father also says this," Cochise agreed. "He says we must have good strengthening food, like the deer meat, or we will grow weak. He says if our women do not have this meat they will not have good milk for their babies. If the babies don't have good strong milk, they won't grow up to be strong warriors, and without strong warriors to fight away those who want our land, we Chiricahuas would soon not exist. I think that is true."

Naretena lifted his thin shoulders and grimaced.

"Yes, I have heard our father talk like that. Of course I know the Mexicans raid us and steal our women and children, just as we raid them and take captives. But we kill Mexicans, and they kill us . . . I do not like all this killing."

"Neither do I," Cochise confessed, then stiffened, pointing out over the seemingly empty desert. "There they are. The Voice spoke truth. Look to your right and far out. See the little puffs of dust rising? A scout is riding ahead of the main body of warriors, if I read the sign correctly."

Naretena shaded his eyes and squinted, but still did not see.

"You do have keen eyes, Brother," he said. "I don't see the dust yet, and neither does the sentinel. Perhaps he is taking a nap in the shade."

But at that moment there was a warning coyote call from the peaks, and the brothers laughed. They knew that the sentinel also had spied the puffs of dust and was telling the people in the encampment that they could get ready for the return of the raiding party after their foray in the dusty little Mexican villages to the south.

"I wonder what they will bring home this time," Naretena murmured, having spotted the dust himself. "And how many dead Mexicans they left behind."

"Better think about how many dead warriors they bring home," Cochise said grimly. "We are not always fortunate."

"I wonder whether they saw any of those pale-skinned people this time," Naretena said. "They must look queer. I've seen the Mexicans, especially the captive women and children, and they have brown eyes and black hair, something like ours. Sometimes I wonder why we hate them so much. What did they do to us?"

Cochise was intent on the progress of the little puffs of dust that marked the course of the returning warriors.

"Our father told me about that. He said there was a time when there were no other people in all this land except Indians, and mostly Apaches in this country of our own. He said that the old men told him of the coming of the Spanish people. They often had light-colored hair and blue eyes, though many had dark hair. Their skin was not dark like ours, or that of the Mexicans. He said that we did not hate them very much. We let them build their big adobe buildings, where they prayed in their way.

"Tulac was chief of all the Apaches when the Spanish lived here with us. He allowed the Spanish priests — those men who wore long skirts — to take his little son, who is now Juan Jose, the chief, and teach him to speak as they do and think as they do.

"But the Spanish went away, and the Mexicans came in larger numbers, and finally they murdered Tulac, although he thought of them as friends." He added slowly, "And tortured him, first."

"Does Juan Jose hate the Mexicans?" Naretena asked.

"Juan Jose was taught by the priests of the Spanish to love all men. He is kind to the Mexicans and also to the white men with the hair-faces — the Americans, they call themselves."

Naretena shuddered.

"Hair-faces! I hope they don't come here. . . . Was it a long time ago when Tulac was killed?"

"I think it was. Juan Jose was a very young man then, and now he is of our father's age and growing old."

Naretena looked up into his brother's lean, large-nosed face, and tears moistened his eyes. Struggling for composure, he looked away into the sun-shot distance.

"Why are your eyes going far away?" Cochise asked, more gently than was his ordinary habit. "Is something making you sad? Do you see something I do not see? What is it?"

"You will soon be going on your first raid," Naretena mumbled.

Cochise laughed.

"Why not? I want to be of use to our people, and I am old enough to go. I have expected to be called for many moons. . . . But why do you say that? Have you overheard something?"

"Our father is working on a bow — a hickory bow," Naretena said. "It is for you."

"It could be for Juan, or even for you," Cochise teased.

Naretena refused to be amused.

"It is for you," he declared. "Is not your name Hickory Wood?"

Cochise ignored the question. Everyone knew his name.

"Did our father say it was for me?"

Naretena shook his head.

"No, but I know it is. Soon he will give it to you, and after that you will go on the raids. I shall not like to see you ride away with the warriors, my brother. I shall not like to look into your eyes when you come back, having killed someone, even though he is an enemy of the Chiricahuas."

Cochise did not like this talk. He shrugged and

waved the thought away with a sweep of one long-fingered hand.

"We must live like men," he said, his lips coming together in a straight line. "Even if it means war with those who steal our country and kill our game. Surely you do not want me to be a coward."

Naretena took a long breath, his face glowing with admiration.

"You will never be a coward," he declared.

Cochise knew that it would be hours before the raiding party could cross the desert valley and climb the slopes of the mountain to the Stronghold. He suggested that Naretena return to the encampment below and rest in the shade. Unwillingly, Naretena agreed and ambled away. Left alone, Cochise relaxed, enjoying the haze-softened hues of the distance. The puffs of dust were larger now. He found a shaded spot and lay flat, cradling his head on one arm.

When he opened his eyes later, the shadows of the saguaros were lengthening. A roadrunner, flashing past with stiff crest erect, gave him an angry-eyed glance that brought a smile to his lips. A turkey hen spoke anxiously to her poults, and

Cochise caught a glimpse of her and her young ones as they slipped silently through the trees on the steep hillside, bound for their roosting place. Quails began to call from the mesquite, and a cactus wren perched on a yucca spike to eye the human being suspiciously before flitting off to his nest in a nearby saguaro.

Eventually, the Chiricahua braves on their jaded mounts became visible, advancing slowly in single file, Cochise's father leading on his gray horse with the spotted hips. Although Cochise looked closely, his eagle eyes could not determine what the packhorses held. He thought of the women down below, and he hoped that the burdens would not bring sadness and mourning to them. The sights and sounds of mourning were all too familiar to him. Raids often resulted in tragedies for the raiders as well as for those raided. Staring at the gradually approaching riders, Cochise hoped that all who rode out had returned unharmed.

When they were still far below him, on the steep slope that would bring them finally to the cleft in the rocks that was the entrance to the Stronghold, Cochise's keen nostrils caught the odor

of equine sweat. His ears heard a man call out to another, and he detected the answer, although he could not distinguish the words.

The scout, urging his horse, was almost up the grade and soon lost to sight among the rocks. Cochise's father was not far behind, sitting erect in his saddle, his feathered lance in one hand.

Cochise jumped to his feet and raced back down the trail, jumping from ledge to ledge on strong legs, and zigzagging easily past rocks and trees. From overlooks along the trail he glanced down at the encampment, noting that Indian ponies were feeding on the green grass beside the stream. Children were playing and women were busy over their supper fires, the smoke of which was pleasant to his nostrils as he ran.

From that height everything below was in miniature, for the great rocks reached up to heights of two and three hundred feet on all sides of the valley, making it a simple matter to guard the encampment against enemies. There were those who had tried to gain an entrance, but all had failed, for vigilance was kept at all times, and sentinels could see for miles around.

Cochise was proud of this record, because

men of his blood had served as Chiricahua leaders for three hundred years.

In that valley, many of the Chiricahua leaders believed, one felt the presence of the Great Father, and also that of White Painted Lady and her gifted son, Child of the Waters. For that reason very few of the tribe would, of their own accord, live anywhere else.

The trail led down from the lookout through stands of hickory, ash, oak, and other smaller timber, and at last through aromatic sagebrush. The leaves of sagebrush were used as medicine and in many other ways, including the production of "ghost medicine." This was the billowing black smoke through which the Chiricahuas walked for purification after being in contact with dead bodies.

Cochise was in time to see his father ride through the cleft and advance, stern-faced and unsmiling to the center of the encampment. With long strides Cochise arrived beside his father's horse just as the chieftain brought it to a halt and then lightly dismounted.

There were no words of greeting between father and son; merely a pleased exchange of glances as Cochise took the bridle reins and led the horse away. His father, meanwhile, turned toward his wickiup where his wife awaited him.

Sensitive to the pleasure of animals as well as to that of human beings, Cochise stripped the Mexican saddle and the horsehair bridle from the tired horse. Then he stood watching while the animal rolled in the dust, got up, shook himself, and set off for the stream, a drink, and a feast on the green grass.

One by one the other warriors entered the valley to be greeted by wives, fathers, or sons, and at last the packhorses were driven in.

"Look!" Naretena murmured to Cochise. "Captives!"

It was not good for Apaches to stare at the captives. The boys pretended indifference, merely glancing at the packhorses and then quickly away.

A woman rode the last pack animal — a young Mexican woman. Her feet were tied together beneath the horse's belly. She clutched a little boy to her breast, and behind her, on the animal's back, a little girl hid her face in the woman's blouse.

Her captor allowed her to remain on her horse

while he saw to the disposition of the plunder packed on the other pack animals. Then he cut the thongs that bound her, grabbed her roughly by the elbow, and dragged her from the horse.

She fell in a flutter of bright skirts, but she did not cry out, although the two children, who were still clinging to her, screamed pitiously.

For a moment the woman lay still on the ground, seeming to be stunned from the fall. Then she sat up and pulled the children into her embrace, her huge, frightened eyes darting from one Chiricahua countenance to the other and finding only blank disregard. No sympathy, no warmth was shown her. She was an enemy — one of the hated race and therefore beneath contempt.

From the time the sentinel's warning had sounded, the women had been busy preparing for the homecoming of their men. The air was filled with the good fragrance of roasting meat for the appetites that were to be appeased.

While they waited for the food to be served, the young braves strutted around, showing off before the young girls, and bragging about the spoils of the raid and their part in the affair.

Cochise, listening and thinking of the time when he would be returning from a raid, heard Gokliya, a fat youth slightly older than himself, say, "I outwitted those Mexicans. They had to realize I was one clever man. All the girls wanted me to capture them and take them home with me, but I didn't want my horse to get tired carrying them, and I was afraid they were too weak and skinny to walk so far."

Naretena's eyes opened wide.

"Is that the way it is?" he whispered. "Do the Mexican women *want* to be taken captive?"

Cochise's lip curled contemptuously.

"Of course not," he said. "Gokliya is lying, and I despise a liar. Come away from him. One cannot trust him."

There were no injured men to be considered and no deaths to darken the spirits of the people in the encampment. After the feasting there would be the recounting of the excitement and the perils of the excursion. Then there would be dancing. Everyone would take part in the fun.

The fire was kindled. The relaxed warriors gathered around it, the chief and his headmen sitting together on blankets near the fire, the younger men congregating a little distance away, where they could talk quietly and enjoy their own version of the raid. The women and the children made up another group, a splendid audience for the men who enjoyed telling and retelling stories of the adventure as much as the stay-at-homes enjoyed hearing them.

Cochise's brothers watched every gesture and listened to every word with the deepest interest, but he sat unmoved. This, he could see at once, had been an easy victory, and nothing to brag about. The Mexicans had been few in number, their able young men off on a hunt somewhere, and the old men too frightened to do anything except run away, taking their families and leaving the village to the invading Chiricahuas.

The young woman's captor told how he had found her asleep and had slung her over his shoulder and walked away with her. She had fought him like a wildcat, he said, showing scratches and red lumps to prove how she had bitten and scratched him, but he had tied her to the horse and had let her scream while he went back for the children.

Cochise darted a glance at the woman. She sat

like a statue, the children's dark heads in her lap. They, worn out with the ride in the heat, the terror, and lack of food, were asleep.

There had been other captives, but these had been released when it was known that they were ill. The Chiricahuas did not want to bring illness into the encampment. It made no difference to them that the released captives might not be able to reach their village, but would die in the desolation and heat.

This young woman was healthy and fine looking, Cochise could see. She would be taken by some Chiricahua who wanted a wife. As for the children, the Apaches were fond of the little ones. They would be given to women who had lost children or who could not have them. The boy would grow up as an Apache, riding, raiding, hunting, as other warriors did. The little girl would learn woman's work.

Should no warrior want to take the woman as his wife, she would be given to some Chiricahua woman to serve as a slave and to do all the hardest work of the encampment.

The moon rose and looked down on the encampment. The Apache women had gathered up their little ones and had carried them off to bed. Some of the older children slept, sprawled on deerskin robes or blankets purloined from the Mexicans. The young women, seeming to have endless energy, danced on to the beating of the drum and the songs of the assembly. Now and then a group of braves dashed in with short yips of enthusiasm to do their leaping, stabbing dance while the bullroarer was whirled in the night air.

No one had gone near the Mexican woman. No one had thrown her a bone to gnaw on. That would come later, after the warriors had extracted the last sweetness out of the reenactment in words and dance and song of the raid.

Eventually the fire died down, first into glowing embers, then into ashes that occasionally spat out a sparkle of fire. The older men gathered up their blankets and silently drifted off toward their wickiups. The drum stopped throbbing.

Cochise had been lost in dreams, staring into the dying fire. But now it was time to go to bed. Owls hooted in the timber; coyotes sent their weird cries up from the fastness of the rocks. He got up slowly, stretched and yawned, then shook Naretena and nudged Juan with his toe.

"The moon walks away," he said, "and Grandfather Sun will soon be looking for us. Come to bed."

The boys got up, half-asleep, and staggered away, following him. But before he reached the lodge they shared, Cochise's father called to him from the door of the chief's lodge.

Cochise walked over to him.

"I have heard your call, my father," he said.

His father took a step forward and placed one hand on his son's bare shoulder.

"My son, you are of an age to ride with the men. You will go with us on our next raid. Meanwhile, so that you will be prepared to play the part of a man, I have made a strong new bow for you."

He extended the new bow to Cochise, and the tall boy received it, his heart racing.

"You are already a good shot with your childhood weapon," his father continued. "Now you will build strength into your arms and shoulders, for this is a bow that is not for weaklings. Practice with it until it is as familiar to you as your arms and hands. . . . I would be proud of you."

Cochise stood for a moment looking into the shadowed face of his father and feeling that he had never really known that man.

"I would have you be proud of me," he said.

His father turned away.

Cochise, carrying the new bow, walked rapidly after his brothers.

"I am a man!" he murmured to the sweet night air. "Now I am a man!"

2

A Chief Is Chosen

IN THE PURPLE DAWN of the next morning, Cochise slipped out of his wickiup, bow and arrows in hand, and sought a place of solitude. He wanted no witnesses to his first attempts to use that strong hickory bow.

It was not for a child, he soon discovered. He was a husky young man, but it taxed his muscles to send an arrow flying from that beautifully fashioned weapon of war. His first shots went wide of the mark. He looked at the bow, at first dismayed and then determined. He knew that he would be unable to face his father should he fail to shoot well after a little practice.

The colors in the east changed from purple to pink, and from pink to gold as he struggled to hit his target dead center. His muscles were screaming in agony before he succeeded and, with a great feeling of relief, started back to the encampment.

Stealthily he entered the wickiup. Naretena and placid Juan appeared to be asleep, but Naretena opened his eyes and whispered, "How do you like it?"

Cochise tried to appear unconcerned, as though shooting a new bow were an everyday occupation.

"It is a good strong bow," he said. "I think I shall learn to use it well."

He did not see Naretena's smile, but alerted by some quality in the boy's words, he gave the youngster a sharp look. Naretena had turned away and had closed his eyes again. Cochise would never know from him that he had secretly followed and had seen his big brother's first failures.

Their mother knew the way of warriors—espe-

Cochise's mother

cially young, unfledged ones with new bows. She waited until they were alone, then she beckoned to Cochise.

"I will massage your arms," she said.

Cochise did not argue. Her strong fingers reached into the sore muscles, and the ointment that she used soothed the aches. Without saying so in words, she conveyed the idea that she would not tell anyone about her effort to relieve his soreness.

Cochise's father had called for a day of racing. There would be no more archery that day. Both Juan and Cochise were expected to take part in the competition, as were all boys of their age, and younger. After the racing, they were told to circle the encampment so cleverly that not one set of watching eyes could spy them. Apaches had the reputation of being able to vanish as if by magic, and this was to be the preparation for such a feat.

Cochise was one of the two best runners and was first in the secrecy test. Juan did well for his age in running, but was seen by several people as he tried to make the secret trip around the camp. His father scolded him.

"It was the roadrunner that betrayed me," Juan defended himself when the boys were alone. "No one would have seen me, except for that silly bird. When he saw me, he jumped straight up in the air and squawked."

"You're enough to scare anyone," Naretena teased. "People never see Cochise or me."

"You must learn to distract the bird before it gets near you," Cochise said, laughing at Naretena's quip. "Then while all eyes are on the bird, you must dart off through the brush."

At that moment the sentinel called from the lookout. The chatter and activity of the camp came to an abrupt halt as everyone waited breathlessly for the news.

"Warm Springs Apaches...ride this way. Large

party . . . coming in peace . . . Mangas Coloradas rides at head of party."

A movement of his father's hand alerted Cochise. It meant, "Get my horse and saddle him."

Cochise leaped to obey. Juan and Naretena followed him. He outraced them to the little nook where his father's horses were grazing. Quickly the boys separated the gray with the spotted hips from the others and slipped a rope around his neck. Naretena rode him back to the encampment, and Juan saddled him while Cochise bridled him.

As they watched their father ride out of the valley, followed by half a dozen of his best warriors, Juan said, "I'll race you to the lookout."

Even with Naretena riding on his back, Cochise was not very far behind Juan. Panting, Juan had flung himself, face down, onto one of the flat rocks and, with his chin in his hands, was looking out over the desert.

"I see them," he said. "They are still a good way out."

"Is Mangas Coloradas our friend?" Naretena asked, when he and Cochise were comfortably seated. "Does he want to fight us?"

"He comes in peace, the sentry said," Cochise

reminded him. "He may want us to help him fight someone else, though. Maybe the Comanches, or the Navajos, or the Mexicans. I heard a man say that the Mexicans are working mines in his territory."

"I think this Mangas Coloradas must be a good man to have for a friend," Naretena said, his serious little face turned upward like a flower to the sun of his big brother's countenance. "He is a fierce fighter, the men say. One boy told me that the Mexicans gave him the name 'Red Sleeves,' because he dips his arms in men's blood when he kills them."

"Our father says that is not true," Cochise declared. "He says it was a deer that Mangas Coloradas was cutting up when the Mexicans saw him with bloody hands and arms. But they hate him, those Mexicans, because he is more powerful than they are, and he is such a big man. He hates them, too."

"Not all of them," Naretena said. "He married a Mexican woman . . . I think she must have been beautiful, like the one they brought in this time."

"Aha!" Juan teased, poking Naretena in the ribs. "You've been looking at that one. Maybe you want them to give her to you for a wife, eh?"

Naretena punched back, flaring up in anger.

"I don't want any wives around me," he said. "Besides, Cochise is the oldest. He'll get married first, and after him, you'll have to take the ugliest girl in the camp."

"Stop quarreling like babies," Cochise scolded them. "Watch the visitors."

He, Cochise, had been watching them. There were perhaps twenty in the group. The first one carried a lance, and no doubt he was big, powerful Mangas Coloradas, the chief.

"When I was a little boy, this man was already a famous warrior," Cochise told his brothers. "Our father says Mangas Coloradas has a good head for planning wars. He makes no move until he knows, or thinks he knows, exactly what the enemy will do next. Because of that he wins most of his battles, and he has had many."

"Why?" asked Naretena, idly flipping twigs at a lizard that was sunning itself on the rocks.

"Because there is that 'yellow iron' the Mexicans call *oro*. I don't know why they like it so much, but they do. The Americans like it also."

"Are there many of those hair-faces?" Naretena asked. "I think I would like to see some of them."

"Not me," Cochise said positively. "I hope they stay away."

"Why? Would we have to fight them?" Naretena asked, a tinge of anxiety in his voice.

"I suppose we would," Cochise replied. "That is, if they came as enemies. I hope, if they do come, that they come as friends."

"Hah! I'm not afraid of them," Juan bragged. "I'd as soon fight them as the Mexicans."

Cochise stared him down.

"I'm not afraid of them," he said harshly. "But I do not want to be fighting all the time. I'd like to be at peace with everyone. I'd like just to live here in our own Apache-land to the end of my days. . . . But for that good life I will fight to my last breath."

Tears sprang to Naretena's eyes as he thought of his brother fighting and dying.

"But living is so good," Naretena murmured, gaze downcast. "Why do we always have to think of fighting and dying?"

"Because we have to think of living a free life," Cochise told him. "I would not want to be like an eagle tied to a stake. I would not like to be snared like a rabbit. Even an animal fights for freedom, and we are Chiricahuas. We are free. We must stay free . . . And Apache men do not cry. Wipe your eyes."

Juan rolled over, laughing.

"The bow has made you into an old man already," he told Cochise. "You'll be riding with the men soon, and I wish I could go along. I'm ready, too. I may not shoot as well as you do, but I ride like the wind and I'm not afraid. . . . Now the two groups have met," he interrupted himself, staring down into the desert. "See them? They're talking. . . . Ah, now they start this way. It will be interesting to hear what Mangas Coloradas has to say about the mines and the hair-faces and wars in his part of our land."

Naretena slid from his rock to the ground and held out his hands, as he scrutinized his thin arms.

"Unless I get some fat on my bones, I'll never get to go with you on raids. I'm too thin, and Juan's too fat." He looked critically at Juan. "In the running test you always have to swallow the mouthful of water, instead of spitting it out at the end of the race. You'd better do more running and get thinner, like Cochise."

"Juan endures well," Cochise defended his brother. "He's really a very good runner and getting better all the time. I'll be glad to have him ride with me when our father allows him to raid with us."

Juan was pleased.

"So you're on my side for once," he said, smiling. "I'm going back down to wait for them."

When Mangas Coloradas rode into the encampment, the eagle feathers on his lance fluttering in the breeze, he wore a straw sombrero on his head, felt-soled shoes shipped to Mexico from China, leather leggings, and a breechcloth. Over one massive, muscular shoulder a red Navajo blanket was folded and draped, and his hair was tied in a bundle at the nape of his neck.

Cochise, who had come down from the lookout as the visiting group arrived, stared at the famous chief of the Warm Springs Apaches, amazed by the man's look of extraordinary power.

Mangas Coloradas had a huge body, strong, long arms, great, broad legs, somewhat bowed, and an enormous head. His black eyes were wide and well-spaced, and his very glance was as penetrating as steel. But balancing the power of him was the sensitive, well-shaped nose and the mouth

Mangas Coloradas

that showed humor in its curve. And he was young, perhaps thirty-five, and in every way vigorous.

Seeming to feel the close scrutiny of the tall and slender Chiricahua lad, who stood with arms folded across his chest, Mangas Coloradas turned his gaze in that direction. His direct and piercing glance seemed to gather the youth up, weigh him, and find him worthy. He smiled, and for one breath-taking moment Cochise's eyes met his.

Later in the day Mangas Coloradas made it a point to stroll over to Cochise. In a friendly way he said, "You have grown much since I last saw you. Now you are a strong young man. You will be a good leader of your people when your time comes. I like you. Let us be friends."

He extended his hand. Cochise responded. The touch of fingers — for the Apaches did not shake hands — was casual and brief, a mere brushing of the palms together, but the contact of flesh against flesh was electrifying to Cochise. The memory of that instant would remain forever in his mind.

So would the fragment of conversation he overheard later.

His father and Mangas Coloradas were discussing their families and their welfare when Mangas said, without particular emphasis, "I have a young sister who is ready for marriage. She has been well trained and will make an excellent wife for some young man. She is a quiet girl and one who will brighten her husband's wickiup."

"I should be glad to welcome such a young woman as the wife of a son," his father declared.

Cochise knew, with a shock of his senses, that he was the son of whom his father spoke. Such talking was not done idly and he had a feeling of terror. Were they planning immediate marriage for him? He was not ready for that, and he wanted to choose his own wife when he was ready.

Suddenly he felt much older and ill at ease. Manhood . . . marriage . . . fatherhood . . . He was not ready for that full role as yet. Those responsibilities seemed too great to be shouldered. He did not even want to think about a time when he would head a household. He dashed over to his wickiup, took his bow and arrows, and ran back into the woods.

In the shaded quiet his heart stopped racing, and he could think of less disturbing phases of life. He knew where wild turkeys fed. He had seen young gobblers strutting there only the day before. One of them would be welcomed by his mother for the family dinner.

Quietly he worked through the brush, keeping a screen of it between him and the spot where the birds might be found. There they were, feeding — a hen, some poults, and the three young gobblers. He watched them for a moment, enjoying the natural grace of them. Then, as one left the others and started to fly up onto a branch of a nearby oak, he sent an arrow zinging through the air.

The gobbler, its feet about to grasp the branch, fell in a flutter of feathers, and the other turkeys fled, losing themselves in the tall grass and the brush of the area.

Cochise picked up the bird, feeling no pride in

the killing, and carried it to his mother.

Again he was drawn to the place where his father, Mangas Coloradas, and other headmen of the two Apache bands sat "blowing the cloud" from their stone pipes, their dark faces grave as they discussed tribal affairs.

Delgadito, a brother of Mangas Coloradas, was speaking.

"My Mexican friends tell me that much 'yellow iron' has been offered for Apache scalps. Those men in Sonora want the Santa Rita mines and the copper ore that is being taken from the mines there."

Cochise's father raised his head and stared long at Delgadito, probing the other man's eyes to be

Victorio

sure he was speaking the truth.

Delgadito's brother, Victorio, took up the story.

"There is a white man living near Juan Jose's camp," he said. "His name is Johnson. He has a trading post and is all the time taking gifts to Juan Jose and his people. I think he pretends too much to be friends. I suspect him. But Juan Jose's people like him. They give him presents of fruit. They invite him to their *tiswin* parties."

"We have told Juan Jose to run that man out of the country," Mangas Coloradas declared. "Better yet, to kill him and burn his store. One white man brings more white men. There are too many now."

There was a long silence while Cochise's father considered the subject.

"We are not at war with the Americans," he said finally. "We do not want to be at war with them. They are our friends, for they are fighting the Mexicans. Juan Jose is a capable man. He takes care of his own people. Let it be so. As for the Mexicans, let them try to take scalps. We have many fine warriors, and more growing up."

He looked up, meeting Cochise's gaze, and again Cochise felt those little prickles of excitement race over him.

Excitement was his daily fare during the four days of the visit, and when Mangas Coloradas rode away, Cochise felt a sense of loss and loneliness which he could not explain.

Cochise mastered the new bow. He could send an arrow straight to its mark, even from the back of a running horse. He could run for miles, holding a swallow of water in his mouth the whole way and not swallowing it, no matter how dry his throat became. He could slip in and out of gullies, through undergrowth in the forest, from rock to rock in more exposed territory, and not disturb the rabbits and roadrunners. He had passed all the Apache manhood tests and was ready to go with the other braves on the next raid.

It was no surprise to him when his father said, "You will ride with us in the morning."

"I am ready," he replied.

"Understand that you will be the least among the many," the stern old man said. "You are to serve the others, doing exactly as you are ordered, no matter what you think of them or of the orders. Your duty is to obey, not to win the war; to stay where you can be the most helpful while the more experienced men lead the raid. Watch out for your own skin, lest bullets pierce you or you dash in front of one of our arrows. And be ready to protect our men and avenge those who are killed."

"I will do as you say," Cochise promised.

Juan stepped forward and waited for his father to recognize him.

"I am strong," he said. "I do not shoot so well as Cochise does, and I cannot run quite so fast, but my heart is good toward our men. I will obey orders. May I go this time?"

Their father's face softened.

"Soon enough, your time will come."

"I envy you," Juan told Cochise, as they walked away together. "Why wasn't I born first?"

It was Naretena who suffered when Cochise mounted his horse and rode away with the raiders the next morning.

He said no words of farewell, but his eyes seemed to be sending the message: "Come back to me, my brother."

Two days later, when the raiding party came home, Naretena raced to be the first to take his brother's bridle reins.

"Did you do that thing?" he asked at once, his face anxious.

"What thing?" Cochise asked, although he knew very well what Naretena meant.

"Did you take lives?"

Cochise looked off into the distance, remembering the heat of the very short encounter with Mexican soldiers.

"I don't think so. It was not much of a fight. They charged us; we rushed them; they turned and ran. We followed them a little way, but we could see that they were trying to lead us away from the village, so we turned back and took what we could find in the village. There was not much. I think we have more than they do. There was a little corn. Some dried meat — deer meat, too, so we took all of it. . . . I like the shooting sticks they call guns. I shall have one some day and learn to shoot it well. Guns are better than bows and arrows in warfare."

Naretena sighed.

"I'm glad it was as you say. I shall not want to see the look in your eyes after you have killed a man."

Cochise laughed and gave Naretena a playful push.

"You speak foolishly. A bullet nicked my horse's ear and made it bleed. It is a good thing that he was not running faster or the bullet would have gone through my middle." He grimaced, rubbing his stomach. "I would not have liked that very much."

Naretena did not laugh. He stared at Cochise's stomach as though he felt surely the almost-bullet had left a mark.

Cochise laughed again.

"Come now, Little Brother. Don't look so frightened. I lost no blood, and a man must be a man. I am a Chiricahua. We have much blood in our bodies, and can spill a little without worrying."

"I know," Naretena admitted, wetting his fever-dry lips, "but it will be such a long time before I shall be a man and can go with you. When I grow up, I shall ride beside you and see to it that no one shoots you."

"I'm sure you will be a good man," Cochise consoled him, "and even if you cannot be a warrior, you can be my friend and adviser. You are a very wise boy. I think you will be one of our wise men and of more use to us than warriors. I like to talk with you, even now. . . . You must eat more good red meat so that you will be stronger and the fever will leave your body. . . .Then you can practice with my new bow."

The years sped past. Like Cochise, Juan passed his manhood tests and began to live the life of a warrior. Now and then he and Cochise joined the younger boys in a game of hoop-and-pole, but it became too easy for them to win. During the winter months they played a game with sticks and a puck made of deerhide; or sat in the wickiup and played cards with bits of painted horsehide; or hide-the-bone; or the moccasin game, just to pass the time away until better weather came.

Always foremost in the minds of the older boys was the thought of riding forth to raid and to terrify their enemies. They were trained for warfare from boyhood, and their superb bodies cried out for the release of action.

Although Juan and Cochise had sometimes quarreled when they were growing up, they became much attached to each other and rode side by side in raids, each seeming to know what the other would do. It was on one of these forays into Mexico that they saw a Mexican soldier shoot their father

at the very moment his arrow left the bow to kill one of the soldiers.

As their father crumpled and fell from his horse, the boys raced to his side, calling to Gokliya, the nearest of their warriors, to help them.

"Lift him up in front of me," Cochise instructed the other two. "I shall take him home. He still lives. The wound is deep, but perhaps the medicine man can keep his spirit from going away."

With Juan and Gokliya preventing the enemy from following after him, Cochise goaded his mount into a run, keeping up the pace until he felt it safe to slow to a walk.

Suddenly his father rallied, raised his head, and said, "My son, the time has come. You will take my place. You will . . ." His voice trailed off into a groan, and fresh, warm blood gushed from the wound and ran down Cochise's bare arm.

Cochise felt the blood and the sudden limpness of the man's body, and he feared that his father's spirit had already taken flight. But a pulse still throbbed in the chief's neck. Cochise rode on, hoping that the wound could be healed, and giving no thought to the impending change in his own life, should his father walk the spirit trail.

While horse and rider were still miles away, the sentinel had recognized the horse. He knew that someone was bringing home a dead or wounded member of the raiding party. As they drew nearer, Cochise raised the lance which his father always carried. But it was not until they started up the grade to the cleft that it was known which of the two was wounded — father or son.

Men came to lift the chief gently from the panting, trembling horse and to carry his limp body into the wickiup. There the medicine man, hideously painted to scare away the evil that was threatening the chief's life, waited with the trappings of his trade — the painted gourd, the fetishes, the drum, the tiny fire that was filling the dome-shaped shelter with the healing scent of sage.

After the first examination of the wound and the binding of it with feathery white sage leaves, the medicine man began a weird chanting, accompanied by the rattle of the sage gourd.

Cochise went up the creek to a secluded pool and bathed, being sure to wash away all the blood from his father's wound. As he bathed, the impact of the situation burst upon him.

If my father dies I shall be chief of the Chiri-

cahuas, he thought somberly, adding, *unless the people find me not worthy.*

Naretena came and sat on the bank of the stream, his face sad.

All night the din continued. The medicine man chanted, the seeds hissed in the gourd, the drum sent out muffled throbbings, but just before dawn there was a stillness. Those who were awake knew that the chief had died. The wailing began.

Cochise's mother cut her hair above her ears and removed her red paint and red headband, then put on the dusty black of mourning. Cochise, Juan, and Naretena also observed the custom. While the camp mourned, the body of their chief was washed and prepared for burial; his face was painted red and yellow, and all his jewelry, fetishes, and other belongings were gathered for burial with him.

The grave had been prepared by old men of the tribe. When all was in order, his body was lowered into it and his weapons, his treasured chieftain's lance, his choice amulet of turquoise, and all else he had loved and used, were laid beside him. His sorrowing wife came with a bowl of ground corn, to be placed in the grave so that the spirit might not wander in hunger while finding its way into the spirit world.

While the grave was being covered, the chief's horses — the two he most valued — were led to the graveside. Their jugular veins were cut and their blood was allowed to gush out above the chief's body, as a last tribute to him.

When all was done that could be done for the dead man, his wife sadly set fire to their wickiup and moved to the other side of the valley. For twenty days the camp would be in mourning.

Juan, returning with the raiders after his father had been buried, at once went into mourning, as had the rest of the family.

"Now you will be chief," he told Cochise.

"I am not chief until the council decides that I am worthy," Cochise reminded him.

"You are worthy," Juan said.

"Yes," Naretena echoed. "You are worthy."

"You are my brothers," Cochise said, his sternness relaxing into a fleeting smile for them.

The construction of a new wickiup was not difficult. The Apaches, as they had done for centuries, simply cut a number of slender poles and placed them in a ten- or twelve-foot circle in the ground, then brought the ends together and tied them with rawhide thongs. Over this domelike skeleton they tied bundles of brush or grass, tightly bound, covered the structure with deerhides, canvas, or blankets, and it was ready for use.

A hole was left in the dome, and through this, smoke from the fire pit in the center of the "house" was supposed to drift. However, the prevailing winds did not always cooperate, and the occupants of the wickiup would sometimes become well smoked before the atmosphere changed.

The wickiup could be built in half a day, with willing helpers, and it was often more practical to build a new wickiup than to clean the old one. When contagious diseases struck a village, all wickiups were burned, a new site for a village was chosen, and new shelters were made.

On the twenty-first day after the burial of the chief, a great fire was built in the center of the encampment. Onto the flames women hurled armfuls of sage which they had cut from the nearby mountain slopes. When the black smoke billowed out, those who had been in contact with the dead man walked in it, purifying themselves and, in this way, ending the period of mourning.

"The ghost of our father will not follow us now," Juan said, when he had walked with Cochise through the blackness.

But Cochise made no comment. He knew what would come next, and he was inwardly preparing himself.

As he had thought, the elders waited only until the mourners had bathed, washed their hair, put on clean breechcloths or dresses according to their sex, and had restored their red headbands, before the council was called.

The camp crier made it impossible for anyone in the camp to miss the importance of this gathering. The old chief was dead, he pronounced, and a new chief was to be chosen.

Cochise sat quietly with Juan and Naretena and other young men while the older men talked. It was a ceremony understood by the Apaches and would take hours of talk and discussion.

One grandfather spoke about the father of Cochise, now walking with the spirits. He told of the former chief's bravery and truthfulness. He told of his fine training by the men and women of his — the speaker's — age.

"We knew, in my day, how children should be

disciplined," he quavered. "We made men of them, and women. None was allowed to sit by the campfire and do nothing."

Naretena cracked his knuckles and sat looking at the ground. *Was the old man throwing slurs at him because he was not strong?* he wondered.

Eventually the men began to talk about Cochise. They told of his prowess with the bow. They discussed his athletic abilities. They told how he had brought game to his mother when he was yet a small boy, and how he had carried Naretena on his back because the boy was sick with the cough and the weak lungs.

Cochise slanted a glance at Naretena without turning his head, and he saw how the lad squirmed. It was too bad, but there was no way to stop it. The discourse must go on, and on . . .

At last the fierce-eyed old war chief, who had served for years as second in command, rose to his feet and stood for a moment in silence before calling Cochise to his side.

"We have known this young man since he was a baby on the cradleboard," he announced. "We know what a strong boy he was, and what a fine young warrior he has become. We know how well his father trained him and what his father's wishes were concerning this young man's future.

"We think he would be a good leader of the Chiricahua people — one who would have the welfare of his people in mind at all times. Men of his blood have been our leaders for longer than we can remember." His piercing eyes probed the assemblage. "Is there one who would speak against him?"

There was complete silence. Cochise was accepted. The war chief left him and sat down. It was Cochise's turn to speak.

For a moment Cochise stood with bowed head, overcome with the importance of the moment. He was tall, and of a thinness that made him seem even taller. His face was grave. In lifting his head, he encountered Naretena's gaze. The younger lad was aglow with admiration and affection. In that instant Cochise knew in his heart that whatever his trials, there was one who would never desert him.

"I will never betray your faith in me," Cochise promised. "I will serve you until the end of my days. You are my people."

The lines of his face expressed strength and character. His large, wide-set eyes were steady. The firelight played on the planes of his thin, long face, highlighting the high forehead, the prominent cheekbones, the arrogant nose, and the wide, firm mouth that spoke of a nature which could love deeply and hate with equal passion.

Having done the expected, Cochise turned and walked away. Henceforth he would have his own wickiup. Juan and Naretena would miss him and he would miss them, but his boyhood days were gone. He was a man now, and leader of the Chiricahua Apaches.

This was, he knew, a lifetime task.

3

The Message of the Smoke

COCHISE HAD NEVER SEEN Juan Jose, who had become chief of all the Apaches after the death of Tulac, his father. Juan Jose was a good leader, so everyone declared, and a forgiving man who showed no hatred for the people who had murdered his father.

This was an un-Apache-like trait, but Cochise had been told that Juan Jose had been taught by the mission priests to forgive his enemies, and that he had tried to live according to those teachings. However, Cochise knew there were some of Juan Jose's own followers who feared for his safety and others who resented his Mexican name. In that case, Cochise thought, they should also resent the names of Mangas Coloradas, Delgadito, Victorio, Soldado, and many others who used names of Spanish derivation in preference to their Indian names.

During the visit of Mangas Coloradas, Cochise had heard about the offer of "yellow iron" for Apache scalps, and he had a fear that the man named Johnson was not a good friend of the chief.

Later he had learned that a delegation of headmen had gone to Juan Jose and had asked him not to be friends with Johnson. He also learned that Juan Jose had angrily defended the white trader, saying that mule buyers were coming, at Johnson's request, and that he had promised them feasting and dancing upon their arrival.

Juan Jose had misjudged Johnson. On a day when the warriors and many of the older boys were away on a hunt, Johnson rode into the Indian camp.

"Those Missouri mule buyers are camped at my place," he told the chief. "They're in a hurry. They want to see your mules, and they're looking forward to that feast you promised 'em. How about giving it for them tomorrow night?"

Juan Jose hesitated. The warriors and the older boys would not like to miss the fun of a feast and dancing, but he wanted to sell his mules for the many silver dollars the Americans would pay. And he had made a promise.

"Bring the men to my Santa Rita camp," he told Johnson. "I will drive my mules over to the corral there, and we shall have the big feast."

Delgadito was one of the six warriors who had stayed in camp that day.

"Help round up the mules," Juan Jose told him, "and bring fresh meat, if you find a deer while you are out."

The women and the children in the camp were in a state of great excitement. Johnson had told them about all the pretty things that he was going to bring as gifts when they would have the feast. They imagined the bright calicos and satins, the hanks of beads for headbands and for moccasin ornamentation, the "see-your-face-in-it" trinkets, the white man's sugar and coffee and flour.

Delgadito helped Juan Jose with the mules. The chief sang as they drove the animals into the big stone corral at the Santa Rita mines. His heart was light. He felt secure in his friendship with the white man.

Johnson came to the camp, accompanied by the mule buyers and a man named Gleason, who was to help him with the bloody plans he had made.

"I promised 'em a surprise," he gloated, a sly wryness about his mouth, "and I aim to deliver the goods."

"I'm a mite nervous," Gleason said, spitting tobacco juice out into the sand. "I been thinkin' about

what if your scheme backfires. It'd cost us our scalps for sartin, and I'd sorta like to keep my h'ar for awhile yet."

"It won't backfire," Johnson chuckled. "We'll get old Juan Jose and his gang, collect our money, go home, and live like kings."

"We'd ought to tip off the mule buyers. They'll have a bad time of it if any of the Injuns catch on," Gleason said.

"Nothin' doin'!" Johnson growled. "They'd gum up the works for sure. You just keep your mouth shut and do what you're told."

That night, all innocently, the Apaches feasted their supposed friends. A deer had been brought in for roasting on a spit. Turkey was boiled. Rabbit stew was bubbling in the cooking pots. And there were many pottery jugs filled with the fiery *tiswin* that Apaches liked so well.

After the feasting, the dancing began. For the occasion the women wore their best robes. Fringes swished as the women formed in two lines and danced toward each other and back, singing lustily. The few men left in the encampment joined in, but Juan Jose sat back with the Americans, contentedly smoking. He had seen a little of what was in the mule buyers' wagons. *The women will be happy*, he thought. *This James Johnson is a fine man.*

He had not the slightest inkling of Johnson's plans.

"I 'clare!" one of the mule buyers murmured to another. "I never knew Injuns was anything but murderin' devils. This here Juan Jose, he seems like a right honorable man. A real human bein'."

The next day the men spent most of their time in the corral, dickering over the price of the mules. In the late afternoon Johnson winked at Gleason, and they sauntered slowly to the wagons where the gifts were stored.

"Cut some brush and make us a screen. Can't take no chances of 'em guessing what we're up to," Johnson said. Behind that screen they placed the blunderbuss they had hidden in one wagon, loaded it with the sacks of iron scrap, broken chains, and lead balls the size of marbles. This material, exploded, could be counted on to kill or maim anyone in the immediate vicinity.

The girls and the women were curious. They kept crowding around and Johnson had to drive them back.

"Stay back. Not time yet," he yelled at them.

"Wait a bit, can't ye?" He grinned at Gleason. "See? We're gonna make a real cleanin'."

"I don't like it," Gleason grumbled. "Women and younguns."

"Don't be so chicken-hearted," Johnson growled. "They're only Injuns."

"I'll go saddle up for us," Gleason offered. "I want to get out of here fast, once you light the wick to that cannon."

"Won't be till near dark," Johnson said. "Easier to outwit 'em then."

The women were preparing the evening meal when Johnson decided that the time was right.

"Go tell Juan Jose we're ready," he told one of the little boys. When the chief ambled up, all smiles, Johnson waved his hand toward the pile of flour, pinole, sugar, bolts of cloth, and gaudy trade items, saying, "There it is. You give it out."

To his surprise and annoyance Juan Jose failed to take the bait.

"Oh, no, señor," he said, backing away. "You are the giver. It is you who must present the gifts to the people."

Johnson's temper flared. Everything was set, and here this stubborn Indian was refusing to play his part.

"Aw-w, come on!" he urged, his face getting red with anger. "Pass the gifts around and take your pick first. You know what to give each one. Call 'em up close, so they can see better." He motioned to the women and girls. They rushed up, carrying the babies and the toddlers, the other small children hanging to their skirts.

Still Juan Jose refused to cooperate.

"It is for you to do, Señor Johnson," he repeated.

Gleason saw what was happening.

"Juan Jose," he called, "I've up and decided to buy that favorite mule of yours. Let's go take another look at him."

Glad to have an excuse to evade a task he did not want to perform, Juan Jose went willingly with Gleason.

"Help yourselves," Johnson called to the women, and as they bent to grab gifts which they had been coveting, he touched a match to the fuse and then ran.

When the explosion rocked the area, Juan Jose whirled around and started to run toward the sound. Gleason pulled his gun and shot the chief in the back.

Surprised, enraged, desperate, and probably

already dying from his wound, Juan Jose leaped at Gleason and grappled with him, pulling him to the ground. His knife was poised for the stroke that would have ended Gleason's life when he saw Johnson running toward them.

"Your friend tried to kill me," the chief cried out, "but he is an American, and I am not on the warpath with Americans. If you say so, I will let him live."

A bullet through the chief's head was Johnson's reply.

With Juan Jose dead in the corral, and men, women, and children screaming and writhing in the death agony near the blunderbuss, Johnson and Gleason made their escape.

Delgadito was one of the fortunate ones. With a scream that chilled the blood of the unlucky mule buyers, he led the uninjured men into battle. Only two of the mule buyers escaped. One of them reached Santa Fe, and there he told the story of Johnson's treachery. The other mule buyer eventually reached California.

Within minutes Apache fires were kindled, and news of the massacre went out to the tribes. Sentinels at far points, on the lookout for news from afar, read the message of the smoke and alerted the braves.

On the way home from the hunt, Mangas Coloradas and others of Juan Jose's friends saw the signal and goaded their tired horses into a run. What they saw at the Santa Rita mine encampment intensified their hatred for foreigners of all races.

At the Stronghold, Cochise and Juan were carrying on a brotherly discourse when the sentinel called the news from the peaks.

"Ride with me," Cochise told Juan, then called to his war chief. Soon the Chiricahuas, with their young chief leading the cavalcade, were on the way to a meeting place.

"We will get even," Juan yelled as they rode knee to knee down the hillside. "We will avenge the murdered ones, ten to one."

Cochise's face was a grim mask.

"We will avenge them, but we can never get even. When life is snatched from the body, can anyone put it back? . . . I am eager to talk to Mangas Coloradas."

Guided by the signal fires, they sped through the night and to a meeting with other headmen of the Apaches. Purple dawn lighted the sky when at last all were joined, two hundred Apache warriors with sharpened lances, terrible in their fury, the slashes of red and yellow paint on their faces attesting to their intention to be revenged.

Surrounded by Apache warriors, Delgadito told his story. It was a story that struck deeply into their sensibilities; tore at them; sickened them.

When he had finished, there was a moment of stunned silence. Then a young brave shouted,

"There are twenty-two fur trappers camped an hour's ride away. Let's begin with them."

With animal yips and shouts they kicked their horses into a run and were on their bloodthirsty way.

The American fur trappers were just awakening when they saw the war party; saw what seemed to be swarms of Indians rushing at them. They fought, but not one of them survived, and still the blood lust of the Apaches was not appeased.

When the first fury wore off, the headmen met to decide what should be done about a successor to Juan Jose.

"There will never again be a leader of all the Apaches," Mangas Coloradas declared, leading the discussion. "Let us choose leaders for each of our bands, as the Chiricahuas long ago chose a leader for their own people."

He was chosen to lead the Warm Springs men and women of the eastern territory, while Cochise would continue to be in command of the Chiricahuas in the western area.

With this matter settled, Cochise sent his men back to the Stronghold with Juan as their headman, and he went to the camp of Mangas Coloradas.

As he knew, a marriage between him and the sister of Mangas Coloradas had been suggested long before. He had thought of the conversation between Mangas Coloradas and his father many times, and he had been prompted to visit the older man's camp to see what sort of girl the sister was. But he had been content to be a bachelor until recently, when need of the companionship of a woman in his wickiup began to obsess him.

At the camp of the Warm Springs leader he saw a pretty girl carrying an infant. He had no idea that this was Tesalbinay, the younger sister that Mangas had talked about. He supposed that she was married and was the mother of the child she bore so tenderly in her arms. He was surprised when Mangas said, "This is my sister," and to the girl, "Take the child to its mother and return."

Tesalbinay quickly did as she was told and was joined by two of the chief's daughters, black-eyed, dimpled, lovely girls, whose mother was Mexican.

Cochise looked at them but, in comparison to the Apache girl, he found them unattractive. This quiet maiden would be the kind to do her work upcomplainingly; keep his wickiup clean and his food ready when he needed it. And, from the way she cared for her sister's child, she would be a good mother to his sons-to-be.

When the time was right, he and Mangas talked about marriage. He had found the girl attractive, Cochise said. He would take her home with him if she wanted to go.

Tesalbinay, eyes downcast, shyly agreed to the contract, and wedding preparations were made at once.

While she gathered her personal belongings and rolled them into a bundle to be carried by a packhorse, Cochise had brotherly talks with the massive Mangas, and he found it easy to be fond of the older man. With no one else, except Nare-tena, could he speak his inner thoughts so freely. Their farewell touching of hands was a little more lingering this time.

Several of the Warm Springs warriors accompanied the young couple as they started homeward. The girl looked back longingly just once, then up at her stalwart, stern-faced husband and smiled.

Cochise and his brother-in-law were vastly different. Cochise was a quiet man, seldom joking or laughing. Mangas was a splendid orator with a fully developed sense of humor, though he could also mount to peaks of anger. With his huge frame and massive head he easily dominated any gathering of warriors, but one of his pleasing qualities was the ability to relax into a philosophical quietude, restful to those about him.

Not so Cochise. He had an air of constant alertness, of being forever on guard. He was, in fact, always listening for the inner Voice. He heard it more and more often now, and knew that it spoke truth. His strong face, maturing, seemed hewn out of granite, and his thin lips were nearly always compressed, while his bearing was that of one born to command. He expected obedience, and, above all else, he respected truth. He did not speak with a "forked tongue." What he said, he meant. There was no dissembling. He detested a liar.

On the way to the Stronghold with his bride that day, he felt a great need to talk to Naretena. There were many questions in his mind. Only Naretena was capable of hearing them and giving considered answers.

Safe in the valley, with Tesalbinay shown to her wickiup, Cochise found Naretena and asked him to go with him for a talk.

"I have missed you," he told the small, slender young man with the large, sunken eyes and the hollow cheeks of the consumptive. "Come with me."

Companionably they walked along the stream until they found a quiet spot where a rock jutted out over the water.

Cochise sat for a moment in thought, then he spoke: "Mangas Coloradas says I do too much thinking. He is never followed by the ghosts of those he has killed, as I am. He never feels sorry for what he has done, as I often do. He is happy, where I am sad, and he is able to relax when I remain tense and worried. . . . Now, there is this. He wants to drive the Americans out of our country. He does not want to try to make friends of them. I say they have many good things we should learn about. He says we are better off to go on living in our old way, and that if we do not drive them out of our land, they will drive *us* out, sooner or later.

"I have been remembering things you have said at other times when we have talked, Naretena. I respect your way of thinking. Once you said that the Americans were like rain. First, there are only a few harmless drops to be welcomed; then there is a pleasant little shower to refresh us, but after that, there is a flash flood that sweeps all before it. I think we must make peace with the Americans while there is only that first little shower, some of it good and some of it bad, like this man Johnson. I think we should learn to live as the Americans do."

"In houses?" Naretena asked, surprised. "Closed in?"

"Some day it will come to that," Cochise prophesied. "Our world is changing. I am not old, but already, since I was a small child, many changes have come about. More will come. Some day we shall lay aside our bows and arrows for the shooting sticks of the Americans.

"But, why must they come here, these Americans? The world is a big one. There is room to the north for many people, but they come here and cross our country, shooting and killing us."

"We kill them, too," Naretena said with a sigh. "And I do not know why they come. A long time ago, before we were born, the Spanish came, and after them came the Mexicans. We have seen how other men take over what is ours. They do not respect our rights. They steal from us and offer money for our scalps. They make it impossible for us to like them or to live at peace with them. The Americans will be the same, I think.

"Have you heard how some of our people were invited to eat with the soldiers, and how they were given drinks of firewater, and when they went to sleep, they were killed, every one of them? How can we believe what white men say? Will they keep a promise?

"Yet, I think we must make peace with these white men called Americans, because they are many. Also, they are brave or they would not try to cross our country in the face of our anger. They are foolishly brave, but brave, nonetheless."

Cochise looked into the pool, watching a fish swim idly past.

"They will be hard to drive away, those hair-faces," he mused. "Their guns outshoot our arrows. They have good food and good clothing. . . . But there is something else that keeps gnawing at my brain: They know things I do not know. If we are to live with them in peace, we must learn those things."

"We could teach them things," Naretena said. "Many good things. They laugh at us and our ways, without knowing why we do as we do. . . . But you have a young wife waiting for you, my brother. That is one of the changes you and I must face. She may not like to have you spend so much time with me."

"I need you," Cochise said, "and she will never come between us. Tesalbinay — 'She-Sticks-to-Her-Cradle' — will learn that you are the only one I can talk to when my mind is not resting. How can I tell others that it is in my heart to be a brother with the Americans, when I have come from killing some of them? Yet this is true. I receive this advice from — somewhere. Who is telling me this?" he demanded angrily. "Is it truth? Does this Voice speak with a forked tongue? Tell me, Naretena. Am I hearing truth?"

"When you are still and listen and the words come," Naretena said, "I think you hear truth. These words must come from a good place." He looked away, across the stream, across the pasture land. "Yes, I am sure you hear truth. If only these Americans could know how you feel and how the Voice comes to you, it might make a difference. But they are afraid of us, and we're afraid of them. They lift their guns and begin to fire at the very word, 'Apache'."

He rose and walked back and forth along the stream restlessly, and Cochise rose also and moved off toward the encampment, lost in thought.

"It is this that I find so bad," he said when Naretena walked beside him, "this feeling one way and doing another." For a short distance they walked in silence, then Cochise said, "The men are already growing restless, I suppose. They are only satisfied when they are preparing for a raid."

4

Cochise Plays for Great Stakes

QUESTIONS ... QUESTIONS. As the years passed, one after the other, Cochise counseled more and more often with Naretena. Why did the Americans fight the Mexicans, yet tell the Indians to let them alone? Why was it right for one and not for the other?

"My mind is a corral," he told Naretena one day. "It is filled with wild animals that mill around and around trying to find a way out! Is there a way out?"

"The way out is for you to find," Naretena said, "I would find it for you if I could. I can only tell you to listen more and heed the Voice when it comes. Your heart is right. Someday you will find a white man with whom you can talk about these things."

"But I have waited a long time," Cochise said impatiently. "Many harvests have been gathered, and it is time for the women to plant the corn once again, and still I do not know how to make that peace I have thought about since I was a young boy."

"It would be good to be like our brother Juan," Naretena said, his quick smile flashing as he saw Juan coming toward them, a baby in each arm. "He lives. He does not worry about the whys. He *does*. He does not question."

A little pang made itself felt in Cochise's heart. He had not been so fortunate as to have children. His first son had died, and so had an infant daughter. He longed for a healthy son who would carry on the leadership of the Chiricahuas when his own time came to walk in the shadows.

One day when he had returned from a raid, Tesalbinay was not on hand to meet him and take the bridle reins as he rode into the encampment. His temper was short that day. It was hot. The trip had been useless. Soldiers were everywhere, and it would have been costly in lives of his men to try to rush them.

He slid from his horse's back, let the reins trail, and strode impatiently to his wickiup. When he pushed aside the deerskin door covering, he saw his wife lying on her pallet, a black-haired infant cradled on her arm.

"Your son," she whispered weakly, smiling at him.

His anger vanished. He knelt beside her and gently lifted the tiny form in his arms. Anxiously he searched the little face. The baby stretched and grimaced. To the great pleasure of the watching mother, Cochise laughed.

"My son," he said. "You are a fine boy. But go back to your mother now, little raccoon." As Tesal-binay reclaimed the child, Cochise added, "I live in him. Thank you for giving me this child. Take good care of him."

Tahzay — "Little Raccoon" — was little more than a year old when Naretena returned from a

Tesalbinay with her son

bartering trip to the Mexican town called Tucson, or more often, the Old Pueblo. He had traded tanned deerskins for food supplies and bright dress materials.

"My brother," he said, calling Cochise aside, "I have learned a new thing. The border has been changed. Our country is no longer in the territory untruthfully claimed by the Mexican Government. The fighting between them and the Americans has ended. A treaty has been made, and now our land is claimed by the Americans."

Cochise studied his brother's grave countenance.

"A treaty? We have not been called to sign a treaty. How can a treaty be made without us?"

Naretena looked puzzled.

"I asked that, too. The Mexicans are laughing. They say that the Americans have promised in this treaty to protect them from us. What do you think of that? The Americans we have wanted to be at peace with are on the side of our enemies. If we kill Mexicans, the Americans will avenge them by fighting with us, although before this Guadalupe-Hidalgo Treaty was made, they were enemies of the Mexicans."

Cochise's strong face took on lines of bitterness.

"I do not understand those Americans. They did not ask us to sign a treaty, although this is our land, not theirs. If they could know how I feel about them and the days to come, when my little son will be a grown man, things might be different."

He was squatting on his heels. Now he balled one fist and struck the ground with it.

"This is our land!" he cried out. "*Our* land! Why don't these treaty makers come to make the *yoshti* with me? Or with Mangas Coloradas and the other leaders of the Apache people? Do they think we are dogs, to be booted around as they please? Must we go on forever, fighting for our own country, or will they come, someday, as you said, and sweep us out as by a flash flood?"

"I have made you unhappy," Naretena said, "and I am sorry, but this is a thing you had to know. . . . There was also talk about what the Americans would do, now that they have pushed the Mexicans off to the south. . . . They are already leaving, those Mexicans. You should see them. They have loaded their children and their women into their *carretas* and started south, crying. . . . It must be that they, too, love this land of hot sand and lizards and cool mountains."

"I know what the Americans will do," Cochise said. "They will bring their cattle in to eat the grass and forage our deer need, and deer are to us as cattle are to the white men — food. The Americans will dig in our mountains for the copper and the yellow iron they like so much. What shall we do? Be still and allow them to steal our scalps to be sold to the Mexicans? If they drive our deer away, will they allow us to eat their cattle?"

"Long ago we talked about the possibility of this day," Naretena reminded him. "You knew more answers then, but whatever the answers are now, we shall have to face them. You said then that we must tread the white man's trail or stagger along ghost trails in darkness. All things point to the logic of your thinking. We *must* learn the way of the white man."

"While we are learning," Cochise said grimly, "let them not try to push us out of our own country, or their women will weep."

"And ours? . . . Tucson will no longer be a little adobe town where the people are afraid of us. I was told that soldiers of the Americans are coming soon. Is there word of them?"

Cochise jumped to his feet.

"No. Not yet. . . . I am restless. I'm going to the lookout."

"Shall I go with you?"

Cochise turned. His eyes had a faraway look in them. "No. . . . Not now. I must be alone. I would have the Voice speak to me, if it will."

The Voice spoke to him. Again it said, "They are coming," but this time it was not referring to Apaches — Chiricahuas — returning from a raid. It foretold the coming of ranks of uniformed American soldiers. Cochise understood it that way.

Very little activity escaped the sharp far-seeing eyes of the Apaches. The bloodthirsty braves, remembering Tulac and Juan Jose, took delight in waylaying wagon trains and other travelers of their dangerous, rutted trails. The scattered household goods, the burned remnants of wagons, the bleaching skulls of the westward-bound pioneers marked the trail across the southwestern deserts.

The winking of signal fires in the darkness became a common sight. Men who had camped for the night saw them fearfully, knowing that they told many things: How many in the party; beside which spring they rested; which direction they were traveling. In the daytime puffs of smoke and the flashing of sun on mirrors invited roving Apache bands to descend upon the luckless and do their worst.

The American soldiers had been given orders to kill Apaches, regardless of sex or age. One Indian, they were told, was like another — no good except when dead. After each Apache strike, there was a retaliatory roundup and killing by the military.

The soldiers, however, were often frustrated by the tactics of the Apaches. Once they knew that there were soldiers on their trail, the wily Apaches broke up into small parties, leaving a dozen trails for the soldiers to choose from. When the soldiers split up into small parties, they were easily overcome, and if they followed one of the many trails, it could as well be the wrong one as the right one.

While they floundered at the division point, wondering which trail to follow, the war party of Indians would have regrouped and been on their way, only to resume their diversionary tactics should the Americans seem about to overtake them. Once they reached the folded hills of their own territory, the Apaches seemed to disappear, only to bob up in some isolated Mexican village to wreak their vengeance once more upon the people whom they considered to be their worst enemies.

The Indians had no idea, as they watched from their high pinnacles, that they were witnessing the slow and tortured march of history across their deserts and through their rocky mountain passes.

They had been both puzzled and fascinated by the coming of men riding strange, long-legged, long-necked animals, such as they had never seen before.

Cochise, keeping out of sight of the white men, but seeing everything that went on from a secluded hiding place in the rocks, watched the drivers pack the animals, making them kneel to receive their packs and their riders.

When the riders had gone on into the distance he ventured out to look at the animal tracks. The animals, he realized, had wide-spreading, soft feet that were good for sand but not good for sharp rocks. They chewed their cud like cows, and they had long eyelashes, a hump on their backs, and horny pads on their knees and chests to support them while kneeling. He had no idea, however, that these animals were called camels, or that they originated in North America, many millions of years ago, but vanished from that area with the passing of time and the ensuing geological catastrophes.

Afraid of the soldiers, he did not venture to present himself to young Lieutenant Beale, who was in charge of this camel brigade of the 1850's, but he told Tahzay about them, drawing a picture of them with a stick in the sand.

"They run fast," he told the boy, who was then about eight years old and a sturdy and serious child, "but their feet are not hard, like those of horses and deer. They are so soft that they get sore. I saw blood in spots on the rocks. I think they are no good for this country. . . . I wonder where they came from."

Many of those who had not seen the animals listened with a glint of suspicion in their eyes. Could such devil creatures really exist, or did those who told of them imagine them? Perhaps, some of the skeptics reasoned, those who claimed to have seen the animals had eaten of the weed that causes one to have strange visions. Only seeing the camels with their own eyes could have convinced these people.

It was common practice among the Apaches of that day to have more than one wife. There was much work to be done as a man's family grew, and often a younger woman was chosen so that she might help the first wife.

When it became evident that Tesalbinay would bear no more children, Cochise took as his second wife a pretty, dimpled girl named Nalikadeya — "Maiden Who Walks Along a Ridge" — and she gave him another son, whom he named Nachise — "Oak Wood."

Cochise looked at the baby and felt a pang of fear.

"Things are not as they were when I was a little boy," he told the young mother. "Many changes have come. Many more are coming. I want my two sons to have a good life. I do not want them to spend their lives fighting and killing. I have made up my mind to go to see the chief of the American soldiers and to talk with him. I am not less brave than these Americans. If they will not come to me, I will go to them."

"Will you talk about making peace?" Nalika-deya asked.

"I will talk about being brothers. . . . It has been many years now since the white man betrayed Juan Jose. They killed many of our people that day, but we have evened the score. Times over we have avenged our dead. Now we should forget that thing. It has been like an open wound, festering in the breasts of our people. This has hurt us in our spirit, but it has not comforted those who mourned. I have long known this to be truth. In my heart I know I should go to see the *nan-tan* soldier. The Voice tells me to act now."

"I will ride with you," said ten-year-old Tahzay, who was already a fast runner and a good shot with bow and arrow.

"I, too," said Naretena.

Cochise's glance lingered on those two he loved, but he shook his head.

"It is no place for you. There could be trouble. This must be done carefully, if I am to return alive. Stay here, Tahzay, and watch over little Nachise. When my days are finished, you and Nachise will be leaders of the Chiricahuas, but only if you have made yourselves worthy of leadership. Know now that this does not mean that your people must wait on you. It is you who must be concerned at all times for their health, safety, and happiness. You will be leaders, but your greatest work will be to care for your people, from the tiniest baby to the oldest grandfather. . . . Do you understand?"

Tahzay knew his father's contempt for a liar.

"No," he answered honestly. "But I will try to."

A smile flicked across Cochise's stern mouth, and his eyes softened as he gripped his son's shoulder.

"Then be strong and watchful all the time," he said. "Not just when you think of it, but all the time. Make it your habit. Our enemies increase daily. Soon they will outnumber us. When you find a friend, test him before you accept him. That is a thing Juan Jose did not do; now he is dead. But when you find a true friend, love him. Love him and be faithful, because a good friend is more to be desired than the fastest horse or the best gun."

He turned to Naretena.

"And you," he told the quiet-eyed, calm man that Naretena had become, "offer prayers to Painted Lady and to her Son. Go with me in spirit. I shall feel your presence and be given courage to do what I must do."

Before he rode down the slopes to the American

army encampment twenty-five miles east of the ancient Mexican village of Tubac, Cochise spent much time alone on the peaks above the Stronghold. He thought of the winter and of the comparative peace which the bad weather and the snow had brought. He thought of the quick transition that came over the land with the first warm days of spring, and his mind harked back to the day he had watched for the coming of the raiders after leaving the hoop-and-pole game.

It had been the same this spring, he reflected. There had been the sudden burst of pastel hues, then the more flaming colors, before the sun browned everything. It was blazing that day. Summer had replaced spring. The fruit on the saguaros was almost ready to pick and be boiled down into the syrup the Apache women were so fond of.

Cochise looked down at the desert and felt a great wave of affection sweeping over him. It was as though he feared he might be looking at this great land of his for the last time, and the thought was heartbreaking.

When he felt that he was ready in spirit, he saddled his horse and, attended by Poinsenay, one of his warriors, and a young half-Mexican boy who would act as interpreter, he rode quietly through the cleft on what he hoped would be a successful mission.

He was in no mood to talk. The others respected his silence. And in silence they reached the fringe of trees which screened them from the military encampment.

"Go ahead," Cochise ordered. "Tell them I come in peace."

He sat his horse, ready to race away at the first sign of trouble, since a chief is needed to take care of his people, as he had told Tahzay.

He saw Poinsenay and the boy riding toward the camp; heard the sharp cry, "'Pachee!" and knew how the soldiers would respond to that cry with drawn guns.

In spite of himself, he grew tense, and his eyes darted from bush to bush, noting every detail of the way out of that little stand of trees should a trap seem probable. He knew his capture would bring great honors to the officer in charge of the camp. He was playing for great stakes and trusting that the Voice had not led him unwisely into this situation.

Poinsenay was a brave man. He rode across the

clearing to the entrance of the army encampment with his hands loose on the reins, but he stiffened when he heard the familiar cry, and his eyes were watchful.

"He comes to lead you to Cochise," called the half-breed boy in Spanish.

"Cochise?" That one word was enough to command attention. It was a feared name — a name that struck terror to the hearts of many; a name that brought immediate thoughts of violence.

Major Enoch Steen received the message. He, too, was a brave man. He saw in the coming of the renowned Apache chief to him a possibility of peace. Without hesitation he mounted his own horse and rode to the spot pointed out by Poinsenay.

Cochise came from the trees to meet him, walking his big chestnut saddle horse and looking every inch the chief that he was.

For the occasion he had put on a blue denim shirt and his fringed leggings. His long black hair, parted in the center, was bound by a red band, and on this trip he wore no paint.

His black eyes met the blue ones of Major Steen. In both glances there was suspicion. Each man was weighing the possibilities in this unprecedented meeting.

Major Steen saluted.

"I am Major Steen," he said.

Cochise stabbed at his breast with the fingers of his right hand. "Cochise," he said.

For a moment he studied the major's face. He felt there was honesty in it. He extended his hand.

Steen responded. For a moment their fingers touched, then Steen motioned for him to follow, and he wheeled his horse. Cochise, after an instant's hesitation, followed him to the camp and up to the big tent where orderlies stood ready to take the reins of the horses.

All of this maneuver was strange to Cochise, who had made it his habit to stay as far away from army camps as possible. But he was alert, missing no details, and approving the orderly appearance of the outpost and the quick obedience of the soldiers.

He and Major Steen dismounted and went into the big tent, over which the flag flapped in a strong breeze. Major Steen ordered drinks, but when they were served, Cochise refused his glass.

"Whisky makes blood run hot," he said. "My people have been tricked into drinking, and when they fell over asleep, they were killed. I have not come to get drunk but to offer the friendship of the Chiricahua Apaches. We are not at war with the Americans, only with the Mexicans. With the Americans I am ready to live as a brother."

When his words were translated to Steen, the officer said. "That is good. I accept your friendship."

"It is my desire to learn the way of the white man," Cochise went on. "You know things we do not know. We must learn these things, as little children learn. While we are learning we shall protect American property and lives. We shall also keep Indians with bad hearts out of this part of our country."

"One thing you may not know," Steen told him, "is that a stage line is to be established. It will travel through Apache Pass carrying the mail — paper with talking on it — and men and women as well. There will be a stage station not far from your Stronghold and a store where you and your people can trade. Also, you should know that an Indian Agent is soon to be appointed. He will live at Fort Stanton and will take care of you on your reservation."

Cochise's blood boiled.

"Take care of *us?* Never!" he cried out, stalking toward the door of the tent. "Never will we acknowledge an agent to be over us and tell us what to do. We are a part of this land. We are a part of the trees and the grass and the high mountains and the desert. We are a part of the wind that blows and the birds that fly in the sky. We are a part of the smoke that drifts from our campfires. We are

Chiricahua. This is our country. We will not talk of reservations and agents."

Steen was a cool and diplomatic man. He changed the subject by showing Cochise a map of the Apache country. Cochise was amazed. This was the first map he had ever seen. Once it was explained to him, he grasped its importance. On this big sheet of paper these men had drawn a picture of his country. The springs were marked. The passes were shown. He studied it for a long time, wondering how the white men got this knowledge which they could put down on paper. More than ever he realized that the Apaches must begin to learn the white man's way if they would survive.

"We will protect your wagons when they go through the Pass," Cochise promised. "We will protect the stage station you talk about and the men who will live there. I make you a present of my horse. He is a very good one. I give you my saddle and bridle, also."

Determined to go along with the chief, Steen ordered that a good horse be saddled for Cochise, and the two men parted friends. Experimental friends, perhaps, but at least there had been a certain softening of attitude apparent in Cochise.

Back in the Stronghold Cochise lost no time in telling his people what wonders he had seen and heard.

"Now that I have made friends with the *nantan* Steen," he said, "we will move down nearer to the springs. The sentinels and a few families will stay up here. We will begin this day to learn the way of our white brothers."

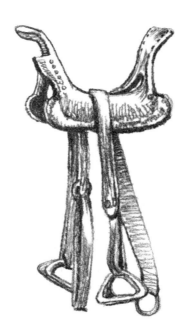

5

Murder at the Stage Station

MAJOR STEEN had spoken truth in regard to the stage line. Only a few days after Cochise had visited the army camp, sentinels at the Stronghold reported that white men were driving stakes and making measurements at Dragoon Springs. Cochise rode down to investigate. Already he felt friendly toward the Americans that he was pledged to protect, although few of them knew of his talk with Steen.

All activity ceased the minute he rode into view, and only the word of Major Steen that they would not be attacked prevented the workmen from preparing to fight it out with the Apache.

"What are you doing here?" Cochise asked in Spanish.

Wallace, the builder in charge, was nervous, but he made no suspicious moves toward his gun, feeling sure the chief was accompanied by able warriors hidden somewhere in the rocks.

"We're getting ready to build the stage station which Major Steen told you about," he answered.

"When will wagons come?" Cochise asked.

"Don't tell him," one man muttered. "He'll meet 'em and wipe 'em out, the sneakin' savage."

Cochise did not understand all the words, but he did get the import of the remark and he stiffened, his eyes angry.

Wallace ignored the remark.

"Be a while yet," he said. "We aim to make a stone corral first to keep the stock in. Then build the buildings."

"Will many white people come?" Cochise asked.

"Reckon so," Wallace replied. "They'll come

in on the stage, eat lunch here while a fresh team is being hooked to the stage, then go on."

Changes! . . . Changes!

Cochise sat his horse for a minute or so, digesting this information, then he pulled his mount around sharply and rode back to the Stronghold. A group of young warriors, including Gokliya, waited for him.

"You are friend of white man now," the stocky, mean-eyed Gokliya said. "We are not. We are true Apaches. We will not be bound by what you have decided without calling us into council. We think you are afraid of the Americans. We will show you that we are *not* afraid."

Gokliya
(Geronimo)

Gokliya leaped onto his horse and, followed by his friends, raced out of the Stronghold, shouting, "Geronimo!" the name he had adopted after being so called during a raid. The word had caught his fancy, and he no longer thought of himself as Gokliya.

A wagon train was coming. Silas St. John, a Butterfield stage line official, and William Buckley, who was to help St. John to build the station and the other buildings, were with the train. Gokliya decided to take advantage of this to show his disdain of Cochise, but Cochise knew his tricky nature.

"Be ready," Cochise told his men. "Pretend not to notice that he has gone. He knows of the wagon train which is coming this way. He and his party will take a roundabout way and intercept the wagons. But we will cut across and turn them back. We will fight them if they object, although they are our brothers. I have promised to protect the Americans and their property, and I keep my word."

Gokliya acted as Cochise had forseen, but the rebel was no sooner gone than Cochise and his warriors were on their way to foil his plans.

When Cochise confronted them, they pretended innocence.

"We are on a hunt," Gokliya said. "You cannot keep us from hunting for food for our families."

"I can make you stop hunting Americans," Cochise told him. "You have defied me. You have become a true Mexican, like your name. Go live with those enemies of the Chiricahuas. You can no longer live with me. Go! Quickly! . . . Before I kill you."

Serenely the wagon train moved on, unaware that their lives and goods had been saved by the watchfulness and the faithfulness of Cochise, the Indian who — so an American Army officer had told his superiors — was "the worst Indian on this continent."

A site had been chosen for a new encampment nearer the stage station site. It would be easier to keep track of what was going on there, Cochise thought. While the new wickiups were being erected, Mangas Coloradas rode in to sit in council with Cochise.

After the customary greetings had been observed, the pipes were lighted and puffed for a moment in silence. Then Mangas Coloradas said, "I think well of you, Cochise. You have been a fearless leader of the Chiricahuas. I would go with you on any warpath, confident of your strength and good judgment, but I think you are now making a bad mistake. You cannot trust these pale-eyes. They will make promises, yes, but when your back is turned, they will light the fuse, as Johnson did at Santa Rita.

"I need your help. I have asked you before to join forces with me, and now once again I ask you. In the East the white miners are coming in ever larger numbers. They are probing the hills, gouging here and gouging there, for the yellow iron which they call gold. They are foolish about this heavy stuff from the earth, and they will risk their lives for it. Come with me. Forget your promise to that *nan-tan* Steen. Before any more of these white men come, let us clear our land of them."

Cochise looked hard into Mangas Coloradas's eyes. The chief was getting old. His eyes were still sharp, but reddened by too much drinking of *tiswin*. His brain was keen, and his judgment was still excellent in battle, but he was more vindictive, if possible, than ever before. It was his body that showed the worst effects of aging. Once he had been lean-flanked and agile; now his belly was bloated, and his steel-like muscles showed the softening of too much food.

"Your words are sweet to my ears," Cochise told him, "except when you tell me that I should break my promise. As long as the white men do not turn on me, I will keep my promise to the *nan-tan* Steen. The white men have come. They will stay. We must not fight their coming in our minds. We must learn, learn, learn, until we know the things they know. I have heard this in my heart. We must learn to live with them."

Mangas Coloradas abruptly laid aside his pipe. He could not smoke when he was worried.

"You are given to too much thinking," he said, as he had said once before. "This is not a time for thinking. It is a time for acting."

"I could as easily stop breathing as to stop thinking," Cochise told him. "It could be that the sort of action we have known is now futile."

When Mangas rode away, his face set and angry, Tesalbinay said meekly, "I think my brother is very angry with you, but you are right, my husband. You have given your word. . . . Now let the Americans keep theirs."

Cochise had watched the men stake out the site

of the new stage depot. Now he saw them running lines across the desert for the road over which the stagecoaches—vehicles he had never seen—would travel. He was a frequent visitor to the station site, where the huge stone corral, forty-five feet by fifty-five feet had been built, and where mules and horses were even then enclosed.

Silas St. John and William Buckley were at the site one day when Cochise rode over to visit them.

St. John, tall, thin-faced and soft-voiced, was outgoing and friendly. Cochise felt an instant surge of friendship for the man. In his heart he knew that St. John was to be trusted. Buckley was different. He was stiff and suspicious. He looked at Cochise with narrowed eyes and pinched lips.

The three Mexican workmen were understandably on guard and hostile. They stopped working the moment he appeared and clustered together, saying nothing, but showing that they were ready to fight, should this be required.

"You were on the wagons the other day, and Geronimo rode out to attack you, but I kept my promise to the *nan-tan* Steen and drove him and his men away," Cochise confided to St. John. "I have told Geronimo he cannot live with me any more, because he did not help me to keep my promise."

St. John invited the chief to get off his horse and to look at the building that had been almost completed. Neither of them had any idea of the hatred in the hearts of the Mexican workmen, nor of how soon it would flare into bloodshed.

When other construction men came, Buckley took the wagons and drove to Tucson for more building materials. He left St. John in charge of James Hughes, James Laing, William Cunningham, and the three Mexican stock tenders and helpers.

When the Americans went to bed that night in the unroofed station building, they had no idea that the Mexicans were planning to rob and murder them. Sometime after midnight, probably alerted by the noise which the Mexicans made in catching mules and saddling them for their getaway, Hughes got up and went outside, where he was stabbed and left dying as the murderers crept inside the building where the others slept.

Two of the men carried axes, the other one's weapon was a stone sledge.

The sound of the blows and the feeble cries of the unfortunate Laing and Cunningham awakened

St. John. When he jumped up, it was to see Pablo swinging the sledge at him. He kicked the man, driving him backward, but at that moment Bonifacio's ax hit him in the hip.

He slugged Bonifacio in the face, temporarily knocking him unconscious, then he leaped for his rifle, which he had left standing against the wall nearby.

He managed to get the rifle, but as he turned with it in his hand, Guadalupe's ax struck him twice, the second blow severing his arm between the elbow and the shoulder.

Wounded though he was, St. John still managed to knock the ax from his assailant's hands with the butt of the rifle.

Dropping the rifle, St. John pulled his pistol and fired at the men, but missed. The murderers fled, and soon he heard the thud of hoofbeats as they rode away.

He could do nothing for his companions and very little for himself. Hughes, who was outside the building, was dead. The other two, Laing and Cunningham, were grievously wounded. St. John managed to crawl up onto the pile of sacked grain, his pistol beside him, and as best he could, he bound

up his hip and arm in an effort to keep from bleeding to death.

All next day, alternately conscious and unconscious, he agonized, hearing the moans of his fellow sufferers. That night coyotes, smelling the blood, fought over the body of Hughes. The starving, thirsty animals in the corral made the night horrible with their anguish.

The assault took place on a Wednesday night, and it was Sunday before relief came.

A newspaper reporter, with a companion, arrived from Tucson, but seeing no signs of life at the station would not approach for fear Indians were in the building waiting to ambush them. When three wagons of a road surveying party came along to reinforce them, they entered and found St. John in a sad state, his wounds swarming with maggots; Hughes and Cunningham dead, and Laing dying.

Men of the road party included Colonel James B. Leach and Major N. H. Hulton. They dressed St. John's wounds and took him to the hospital in Tucson, where his arm was amputated. In spite of his terrible ordeal, St. John made a remarkable recovery and was soon back at work.

Fortunately, he was able to testify that it was the Mexicans and not the Indians who had done the slaying. When others insinuated that Cochise and his band had been involved in the carnage, St. John stoutly defended them. He liked Cochise. He felt a kinship with the stern, solitary, peace-seeking man who was trying to emerge from generations of primitive darkness into the modern world.

The trading post, residence, and station were soon completed at Dragoon Springs, a passing point for Apaches going to and from Sonora, Mexico, where they frequently raided the villages. It was one of the first penetrations of the Americans into the Chiricahua Apache territory.

Camp Buchanan, in the Sonoita Valley, had been completed the year before. It was the only real fort in the area at that time, but Fort Bowie was soon to follow.

Once the Butterfield stage station was ready for use, the men who were in charge began to consider the need for fuel. There was plenty of timber on the mountain slopes, but as one man pointed out, there were "Lots of Injuns roamin' round there, too." It was a problem until St. John talked

to Cochise, who immediately understood their need and volunteered to furnish all the wood they needed, under contract.

"My men will not like this," he told St. John. "They will say I am making them do women's work."

He knew his men well. They grumbled, but they did not dare to disobey him. For the first time they were working for money — American money.

"Why do this thing?" Naretena asked Cochise, troubled because of the anger it had caused among the warriors. "Will it cause your warriors to think less of you as their chief?"

Cochise's chin looked as if it had been hewn out of granite.

"We must earn the trust of the Americans," he insisted. "We must show them that we intend to live among them as brothers, doing the work that must be done. In this way we may not too soon walk with the spirits, and we can enjoy our land, in spite of the strangers."

"It is the Voice speaking to you again," Naretena said. "You have known this for years, although others of our people think it is foolish."

"It is a new thing for Apaches," Cochise agreed. "They are not used to this way of being paid for what they do. They would far rather go the old way, taking what they want from the traveler and the villager to the south. They do not care to have the good will of the Americans, although they are glad to get the money."

"It does them no good," Naretena remarked. "They gamble it away and have nothing left. And even as they gamble, they dream of the excitement of the raid. How can they learn a new way of life?"

Cochise pondered this thought.

"No one can change my men until they are ready to change," he admitted, his gaze fixed on some far-off object. "The change must not come from the outside, but from their hearts."

"But they do not hear the Voice," Naretena told him gently. "Do not think harshly of them if they are slow. If they could understand that you are trying to save them from that rabbit life called a reservation, they might be less critical of you. Some of them whisper rebellion. They do not know that your kind of softness is a sign of strength. You have not trained them to understand peace."

Cochise looked up. His gaze was sharp.

"You are right, Naretena," he said. "They live for the war paint and the attack. For too many harvests have we lived in this manner. Peace is a thing to learn. We have been at war almost all my life. We have killed many. We have lost many of our men in battle. But the time will come when we will be hunted like wild animals unless we learn to live with these strangers."

"Mangas thinks you are mad to try to be a brother to people who hate you," Naretena said. "He sees ahead to a time when so many Apaches will have walked the spirit trail that none will be left to fight for their rights."

"Sometimes I think he is right, and I am wrong," Cochise confessed. "But the Voice tells me to keep my promise to their *nan-tan*. That is why I told the men at the station that we would bring wood, and we will bring wood, grumble though the men do. For, this one thing I know, Apaches cannot live happily in a cage. The eagle cannot fly with clipped wings. We are a part of this land. We are a part of the sunshine and the storms and the winds that blow. We are free. Freedom is our life. We are like the wild turkey and the fierce-eyed roadrunner. To tie us to a tree would be to kill us. We must know freedom, or life is a nothingness."

But while the primitive, uneducated Cochise was trying to find a solution to one of the gravest problems of the age, many of the men he was trying to befriend misunderstood, and they distrusted him and his motives.

"Give a redskin a chance, and he'll ram a knife through you," one of them growled. "This here Cochise, now, he pretends to be a good Injun, but inside he's like all the rest."

In October of 1858, the first stagecoach bounced and jounced along the new road, going safely through Apache Pass, thanks to Cochise, and stopping for a fresh team at the Dragoon Springs depot.

Cochise, intrigued, as a little boy would be with

the strange vehicle, was there to watch the passing of the novel coach. Far from thankful to him for insuring their safety, the passengers saw him and were terrified. They could imagine the war whoop and the zinging arrows, and they were half-disappointed that the stopover was uneventful.

Winter came, powdering the peaks of the Stronghold, and still peace reigned in the Chiricahua country. With the first warm days of early spring Cochise was besieged by his men.

"There is nothing to do," they complained. "We are no longer men but old women, hanging around the campfire. Let us go on one more raid, to lift our spirits. Since you do not allow us to attack the Americans, let us go south of the border."

So pressed, he agreed.

"Be patient. When the time is right, I will tell you."

Probably thinking they would reinforce their status with Cochise, the white men at the stage station invited him and some of his warriors to the trading post where they had made a display of gifts from which the Indians might choose.

The eyes of the Indian men glittered as they saw the good hunting knives, the blankets, the silver bridle ornaments, and other gifts laid out for them. But they were careful, cautiously examining the area around the gifts for fear the Johnson episode might be reenacted.

Cochise took nothing. Instead, after all his men had made their choices, he walked over and tossed a handful of gold nuggets onto a blanket.

Instantly the Americans were filled with excitement.

"Where did you get this gold?" they asked. "Is there much of it?"

Cochise thought less of them because of their interest in the "yellow iron," as he called it. One could neither eat it nor wear it, so why be determined to store it up?

"It is in our hills," he told the men, with a sweeping gesture of one hand. "In many places it may be found. Where these chunks came from, I have forgotten. Now and then I see the yellow glint of it, and I pick it up, but it means nothing to me. I do not dig for it."

With immense dignity he turned his back on the gifts and the gold and stalked out.

"He knows where he got it," one of the men

muttered to another bystander. "He knows. He jist ain't tellin'."

"I'd worm it out of him," the other man said, staring after Cochise, "if I had him out somewhere alone."

"I wouldn't advise you to try it," Wallace, the station manager, advised the man. "He's quicker than a streak of lightning when he's stirred up. Don't take him for a fool."

As he had promised, Cochise ordered a full-scale raid that spring, when — to his way of thinking — the signs were right. Though Tahzay was still rather young, Cochise provided him with a spear and a knife and arrows for the good bow he had fashioned earlier for him as his oldest son. Then he told Tahzay to be prepared to go out with the warriors.

"You are my son," he told the boy, as they rode southward through the awakening colors of spring, "but do not expect favors on that accord. As my father long ago told me, it will be your duty to assist others. Do as you are told. Do not question the judgment of the other men. They have been on many raids and know what is to be done. No matter how difficult they make the trip for you, say nothing. It is your manhood they are testing. How severe the test will be we cannot know until the raid is over."

Neither he, nor any of his warriors, expected the resistance which they encountered from the sleepy little adobe-walled town in the hills of northern Mexico. Riding fresh horses and armed with good firearms and plenty of ammunition, a contingent of Mexican soldiers charged out to meet them.

The battle was short, and in it there was no satisfaction for the Chiricahuas. Mexicans were killed, but so were Chiricahuas.

Many were wounded, including Cochise, whose wound was painful but not serious. Plunder was taken, although not much of it, and Cochise rode home with a fine double-barrelled shotgun with engraved silver on its receiver.

The men had worked off some of their pent-up energy, which they could further expend by digging graves for the dead men and boys that they carried home with them.

The word was sent ahead with a scout, and the encampment was in mourning when the war party returned. There was no celebration that night, and the sound of mourning that greeted the returning warriors was enough to make even the most vainglorious warrior keep silence.

Tahzay came to his father's wickiup after Tesalbinay had bound the chief's wounds and had made him comfortable.

"I am proud of you, my son," Cochise told him. "You behaved well, and I am glad you were not among those injured. When you rushed to the rescue of your cousin, Juan's oldest son, I feared for you. Then I saw how well you handled your horse and how expert you were in dodging bullets, and I told myself that you would live long and be a great leader of our people when you take my place."

Tahzay bowed his head and said nothing, pleased though he was with his father's approval.

6

The Making of War

REPEATEDLY MANGAS COLORADAS begged his brother-in-law to forget his peaceful ways and join him in trying to exterminate the Americans. There were many more Americans in Apache-land as the years rolled past. As Cochise had said, there was no end to them. With increasing numbers of Americans, the Apaches were beginning to be less effective, although they were still feared.

Mangas had reluctantly come to the conclusion

that it was good policy to be on good terms with them, and in the spring of 1858, he made one of his first major mistakes in judging them. He thought the miners at his Santa Rita mines had a good feeling for him when, as one man said, "They merely tolerated the old scamp."

In spite of his former intense pride, he stooped to attempted bribing in order to cadge favor.

"Come with me, and I'll show you where the gold ore may be found," he told some of the more important miners. They talked this suggestion over and decided that Mangas intended to get them out one by one and kill them. The idea took possession of them finally, and made them boil with anger.

One day, when there were no other Apaches in the camp, the miners jumped Mangas, stripped the shirt from his huge torso, tied him to a tree, face first, and repeatedly beat him with harness straps.

His back was soon one mass of blood, and after a while, unable to tolerate the pain, Mangas slumped, unconscious.

Delgadito, who was returning from a ride, heard the commotion and slipped into camp to see what was going on. From a hidden spot behind some machinery he saw his brother crumple and retreat from agony through lack of consciousness.

Laughing and chattering in their glee at having beaten the unbeatable Mangas Coloradas, the men left him and went to reinforce themselves with liquor. Raging inside, but acting with extreme caution, Delgadito dashed over to the tree, cut the restraining ropes, and carried the limp form to the nearest spring. There he bathed the slashed and bleeding back with cold water and restored Mangas to consciousness.

"Never let anyone know what they did to me," Mangas begged. "Get me a shirt to cover my shame. . . . Now you see how these Americans are. They pretend friendship, then cut you to ribbons. . . . I am ready to kill all of them. Cochise is wrong. We cannot live as brothers with these men. . . . Take me home, then go for me to Cochise. Tell him we must kill all the men at the mines first."

Before Delgadito could ride to the Stronghold, a strange set of circumstances had overwhelmed the Chiricahua chief.

On a little ranch in Apache-land a white man named John Ward lived with his wife and her son, Mickie. She was a Mexican woman, who had been a captive of the Apaches and had borne her Apache husband a son, who was now the adopted son of John Ward, Ward having bought her from her captors.

One day the boy was out herding Ward's cattle when he was surrounded by a small party of Apaches.

"You are Apache," they told the boy. "Come with us. You belong with our people."

The boy tried to break away, but could not do

so, and was taken away by the Apaches.

Ward and his wife promptly rode to Fort Buchanan and demanded that the American Army send out a detachment to rescue and return the child. This the Army leaders were both ready and willing to do.

Commissioned to undertake the mission was Lieutenant George N. Bascom, a very young and a very arrogant officer, who knew nothing about Indians except that killing them was highly approved.

With a white flag fluttering at the head of the column of sixty men, the detachment rode out, bound for the encampment of Cochise, who — according to Bascom's limited judgment — was the man who held the boy prisoner.

Unaware of the looming problem, Cochise, with his young wife, Nalikedeya; their little son, Nachise; also Naretena and two of Juan's older sons, went to the trading post to spend a few hours trading and talking to the men whom they regarded as their good friends.

They saw the soldiers coming and were curious but not concerned. Was not the white flag a symbol of peace?

Cochise knew nothing of the boy's capture. Free of guilt and secure in his friendship with the Butterfield stage people and white men in general, he did not sense the danger, even when Bascom accosted him.

"I have come to tell you that you must deliver to me the son of John Ward and the cattle you stole, as well," the young lieutenant said without preamble.

Cochise stiffened, and the good nature in his face vanished.

"I know nothing of the boy," he said, "and none of my men have stolen cattle from Ward."

Bascom's lips tightened.

"You . . . lie!" he spat out.

It was the worst insult anyone could have offered Cochise, a man who valued truth above all else. His eyes glittered, his chest heaved, and for a moment he seemed minded to attack the brazen young man, in spite of the guarding soldiers.

"I do not lie," he said.

"That's the truth, Lieutenant," one of the stage operators spoke up in Cochise's behalf. "I've never known him to lie. He's as honest as they come."

"Keep out of this," Bascom snapped. "I'm here

to get that boy, and I want no interference. I'll get him if I have to hang half the tribe. . . . Place these Apaches under arrest," he told his sergeant, "and take them to my tent."

The command tent had barely been erected, and the white flag fluttered above the entrance as the Apaches were herded into the canvas enclosure. None of them had weapons, except Cochise, who had hastily slipped a knife into his breechcloth as the soldiers rode up to the station.

"You are my prisoners," Bascom told them, his young face reddening. "And you will tell me where the boy is, or I'll hang the lot of you, here and now."

"I do not know," Cochise said, his heart filled with fear for his wife, for Nachise, for Naretena, and for his nephews. "If I knew, I would tell you. Free us, and I will try to find out for you."

"You expect me to bargain?" Bascom cried. "With a butcher like you? I warn you, I mean business."

Cochise looked into the angry face of the young officer, his heart crying out at the injustice and folly of the affair. What should he do? He had been trapped, betrayed by that white flag, caged like a wild animal, when he had done no harm to that boy or to this young man.

It was more than he could tolerate. Flight was the only answer. With a terrible, strangled scream of frustration and hatred, he whipped the knife from its hiding place, slashed the canvas as he leaped forward, and was off, zigzagging as the bullets of the guards struck the boulders and ricocheted. Not until he was safe among the familiar rocks, did he know that one leg was bleeding from a bullet wound.

One of Juan's sons had tried to follow Cochise through the slash in the canvas, but had been dropped by a bullet through the intestines. He was dragged back inside the tent, and the others were cowed by the soldiers' bayonets.

In spite of them, Naretena knelt beside the wounded man and tried to stop the flow of blood.

Cochise had been at peace with the Americans for almost five years. He had wanted to stay at peace for the remainder of his life, but suddenly, through the stupid action of a very young man, all was changed.

As he raced into the encampment, he gave a coyote yell that brought the aging Tesalbinay running to his side in a panic. The sound struck the sensibilities of everyone in the camp like the blow of a giant hammer. Instantly, weapons were snatched and readied. Babies were grabbed up by their startled mothers, and everyone waited for the words that would spill from Cochise's mouth.

In a sobbing rage he told them what had happened. Gone was the affable and relaxed chieftain. Even before he found his paints and smeared his face as a man does when he goes on the warpath, Cochise's countenance was terrible in its hatred.

"There is a stage coming in from Tucson," he told his brother Juan, who had raced to be at his side. "Take the passengers captive, but do not kill them. I will use them as hostages. We must barter life for life, or that *nan-tan* baby face will kill our dear ones."

Juan and his friends hastened to obey, but the driver saw them and, putting the whip to the horses, raced safely to the station.

The Chiricahuas were furious. They had forgotten caution in their frenzy of fear for the imprisoned ones. They remembered that there was a wagon train in the distance — a wagon train they were to protect. But pledges meant nothing now. With a wild yell Juan urged his men toward it.

There were two white men on the wagons and eight Mexicans. This time Juan moved with caution in true Apache fashion. He waited until he and his men were hidden by a low ridge, then, as the wagons rumbled up to this position, he gave a terrifying war whoop, echoed and reechoed by his men, and descended upon the surprised travelers.

In minutes the Americans were overpowered, and the Mexicans were tied to the wagon wheels. The wagons were loaded with barrels of flour, but the Chiricahuas ignored it. They set the wagons afire, tied the Americans to horses, and raced back to the Stronghold with them.

Cochise took the luckless hostages to the hill back of the stage station and called down to Bascom:

"I will kill these men if our people are not released."

Bascom had no pity for the innocent travelers.

"Let them go, or I'll hang your people right now."

"Cochise is a man of his word," Wallace, the station agent, shouted to Bascom. "He doesn't *know* where that boy is, and he's desperate. You're forcing him to kill those men who had nothing to do with this affair. . . . Let me go talk to him."

Cochise had forgotten what friendship meant.

He seized Wallace, seeing in him one more bargaining asset. Wallace screamed to Bascom that he
would be responsible for all their lives if he per-
sisted in his madness, but by that time Bascom had
only one thought in his mind: retaliation for the
refusal of Cochise to do as he, Bascom, had
ordered. There was no swaying him with logic. As
Cochise became more and more frenzied, Bascom
became more and more determined to hang the
prisoners.

"The boy!" he bellowed, red-faced and glaring-
eyed. "Surrender that boy or I'll shoot the lot of
you."

In vain the station employees begged him to
relent.

"You'll never get the boy that way," they said,
but he was beyond approach or reason.

His sergeant, knowing full well what it might
mean to his career, undertook to persuade the lieutenant to calm down and be sensible. For that
breach of authority he was ordered court-
martialed.

The argument raged on throughout the hot
afternoon and on into an evening when the desert
wind howled and threw dust in their inflamed

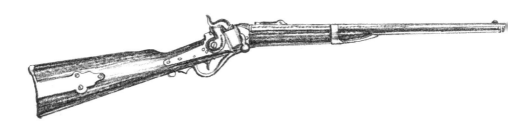

faces, and the keening of the women in the encampment was not unlike a witch's chant.

Finally, with the stormy night coming on, Bascom released Nalikadeya and Nachise, sending them homeward. Then he detailed soldiers to march Naretena and Juan's sons — one of them already fatally wounded — up the hill to an oak tree with strong branches. Ropes were knotted about their necks, and they were suspended, one by one, from the oak tree's limbs.

Cochise was fond of Juan's sons, but he loved Naretena above all men. In a black rage he watched the soldiers kill his brother, then Apache vengeance was exacted: Wallace and the two men from the wagon train were also hanged. They, like the victims of the young lieutenant, were innocent of any wrong. A young man's senseless pride had brought about the death of three Americans, three Apaches, and eight Mexicans.

When the moon rose, blood-red among black clouds, Juan and Cochise crept through the brush of the hillside. From a vantage point they peered at the oak tree and saw the three bodies swinging a little as gusts of wind assailed them. As if the very forces of nature mourned for them, the moon hid its face in the clouds, thunder crashed, lightning flashed, and the rain roared down.

Other Chiricahuas ran with the chief and his brother to the tree, and in silence cut down the bodies. It was Naretena that Cochise liberated. No words were spoken, but as he took the lifeless form of his brother into his arms, Cochise said to himself, "Little Brother! Oh, my Little Brother! I carry you for the last time."

The storm passed as quickly as it had come. Little rivulets tumbled down the mountainsides; the air was fresh and cool; the stars shone with a brilliance unbelievable, and the moon looked down serenely as the dead men were prepared for burial.

It was Cochise who washed his brother's face and applied the paint which would make him known to the spirits. Tesalbinay brought packets of meal, so that the spirits of the three men might have food to sustain them until they had found their way, and Tahzay went to Naretena's wickiup, gathered up his uncle's few belongings, and burned his lodge.

While the bereaved women lay on the ground and beat the earth with their fists, the men were laid in their graves and covered with the earth they had loved. Only when all was done and the others had returned to the encampment, did Cochise lose his icy composure. Alone, he flung himself across his brother's grave and wept.

For twenty days he spoke to no one, but on the twenty-first day, after he had purified himself in the billowing black smoke of the sage "ghost medicine," and after he had bathed himself in the river and put on clean clothing, he told Juan to send messengers to Mangas Coloradas, Delgadito, Victorio, Soldado, Porico, and all the other headmen of the Apaches — even the despised Geronimo — to meet with him for the *yoshti*, the big smoke.

One by one, appearing as though from nowhere, the leaders came. Solemnly they greeted Cochise and sat down to await the others. When all were present, Cochise aroused himself from his black mood and found heart to address them.

"For five years I have walked the path of

the white man," he said. "I have been a brother to them. I have worked for them, and I have seen to it that their lives were protected. My braves have saved them from death at the hands of those of you who hate them. My men have often grumbled about this, but we have learned much from these Americans. We have learned about their way of life and their way of thinking.

"But now . . ." His voice faltered, and for a moment he stood like a statue as he tried to control the emotion that welled up in him. ". . . now the baby *nan-tan* soldier has done this thing to me, and all is changed."

Again he paused, and the tension in him was so strong with hatred that it was almost a tangible force reaching out for vengeance.

"I am no longer a friend of the Americans. I hate them — all of them. I am on the warpath against them."

"That is well!" Mangas rumbled, and the others also agreed.

"I ask you to join me in fighting them," Cochise went on. "For every Apache they have ever killed, I say that ten Americans must die."

The dark faces glowed. Black eyes glittered.

Tahzay

Proud heads lifted. The men were with him in spirit.

He turned to Mangas Coloradas.

"You have asked me many times to join you in killing whites, but I have followed another trail. Now I am ready to go your way. We are brothers because of my marriage to your sister; let us now become blood brothers. Let us mix our blood."

Mangas Coloradas enthusiastically agreed, Tahzay brought a gourd cup and placed it before his father. The medicine man, forewarned, began a ritualistic chanting and drumming. For a time there was no other sound. Then there was silence as the medicine man opened the men's veins, and their blood was mixed.

"Now we will make plans for war," Cochise said.

That war was to last for twelve years and cost thousands of lives.

After the hangings, Cochise and his band had burned their wickiups of sad memories and retreated to the Stronghold, high in the mountains. They could live there for months as in a fortress, safe from harm. There was wild game and clear water; corn in their gardens. With plans perfected, it was possible for them to descend, pounce upon their enemies, and vanish with small reprisals.

Whole regiments of soldiers were sent against them by the United States Government, but with little effect. They were seldom seen. They were like the trees and the rocks — a part of the country itself. Always they seemed to know when soldiers were coming; they knew how to outflank them and to inflict damages without harm to themselves.

"Risk no Apache lives unless that cannot be avoided," Cochise counseled. "Think before you attack. There is no gain in killing five Americans if even one Apache is killed. We fight to win."

He was getting old. Nachise, his youngest son, was as tall as he and a good warrior, brave and steady.

Mangas Coloradas, who always wore a shirt to cover the shameful scars of his beating, was twenty years older than Cochise and had lost much of his zest for raiding and plundering.

Both chiefs, much though they had learned about Americans, were ignorant of the effectiveness of American war methods at their best. Neither of them had ever seen a howitzer, and except for the Johnson episode at the Santa Rita corral, they had no idea of the damage a cannon could inflict. This they were soon to learn.

"Many soldiers come from the west," a scout reported to Cochise one morning. "They head for Apache Pass. Many men walking. Many wagons filled with supplies. Many guns."

Cochise looked out over the desert. The summer heat was at its peak. The sand underfoot was almost sizzling hot. Although he knew that they wore shoes, the American soldiers would find it hard going, he thought. They would be exhausted and all but crazed for water before they could reach the Pass and the cool water of the springs. He decided to ambush them in the canyon.

The Apaches had nothing to work with except the rocks of the rocky mountain passageway. These they put to work. The breastworks they threw up were well positioned. To glance at them one would never suspect that they were not a natural part of the terrain. Inconspicuous, innocent-appearing, they would conceal Cochise's warriors until the exact moment of attack. As the soldiers came nearer, he stationed his men, confident of success.

There was nothing in his experience to warn him that two of the awkward wagons which the horses pulled, were twelve-pound mountain how-itzers.

From a point commanding a good view of the Pass, Cochise and Mangas watched the advance of the wretchedly warm and thirsty soldiers, members of Company E, First California Infantry.

"See how they hurry now," Mangas chuckled. "They smell water, or else their horses and mules do. They are wild to reach the springs."

"They will never reach the springs," Cochise declared.

But he was wrong.

All went as he had planned for a short time. The

advance guard was met by a swarm of arrows from the rocky emplacements. Many fell. The next wave of men fought furiously, determined to reach the springs.

By that time the trained officers had assessed the situation. As soon as they discovered that the arrows came from stone barricades, they sent men around the hills and behind the Apache firing line. Meanwhile, the howitzers were being brought into action.

When the first charge went off and giant boulders exploded and flew in all directions, crushing warriors and blowing some of them to bits, Cochise screamed to Mangas, "They are shooting their wagons at us."

"Order retreat," Mangas screamed back, as the second shot followed with disastrous results.

Cochise complied, but the Apaches were already routed, and as they tried to escape, they were attacked from the rear.

"Surrender!" the Americans called, but the Apaches would not surrender. Instead they fled to the Stronghold to recoup their forces and to plan further action.

Mangas bowed his massive head and mumbled,

"You were right, Cochise. We must make peace, or we perish."

"Not yet," Cochise said grimly. "We will find a way. They cannot overcome us here."

All through the night they watched the Army camp, hoping that a chance for reprisals would come. The first hint of this possibility came just before dawn of the next day, when a small detachment of cavalrymen was sent back to warn other troops coming along that route.

Mangas Coloradas and a few picked men were waiting for them. Only one of the cavalrymen survived the lethal hail of arrows. His horse was shot out from under him, and he was wounded, but he determined to fight to the end. Crouching beside his dying horse and taking careful aim, he drew down on the largest man in the Apache contingent.

The bullet went to its target, hitting Mangas in the breast and knocking him from his horse.

The Apaches lost interest in the fight. Mangas Coloradas was much loved by his men, and two of his brothers were with him when he fell. They turned their attention to him at once, and in minutes had carried him away, to the profound relief of the wounded white man, a private, who

Mangas Colorad

had no idea that he had shot down one of the most important of all the Apache chiefs.

There was a little Mexican army post at Presidio del Jaños, and to that place the Apaches carried Mangas Coloradas. Brushing aside the guards who would have stopped them, they went directly to the Mexican doctor and demanded that he remove the bullet and save their chief.

"If you do not remove it, we will kill you and everyone in the village," they threatened the speedily awakened doctor. Such was the fear of the Apaches that their words were believed.

From the *presidio* to the adobe huts the word spread. It was a time for prayers. Prayers for their enemy, the wounded Apache. Prayers for the poor little doctor who must perform a miracle that the villagers might live.

Happily the doctor was dedicated to his profession and had considerable skill. He removed the bullet, revived the patient, and bandaged him beautifully.

Mangas sat up, groggy, but glad to be alive. Delgadito and Victorio lifted him onto his horse and rode away with him, one at each side.

The villagers took a deep breath and thanked

God for their deliverance. They talked of nothing else for days. A miracle had been demonstrated, there in their own village, and because of this miracle, they had lived to tell of it.

Meanwhile, the Americans had won the battle of Apache Pass, and Cochise, the capable and hitherto undefeated Chiricahua chieftian, had suffered his first defeat.

Now the order went out from the War Department to show no mercy, but to take prisoner all Apaches, men, women, and children, wherever they were to be found.

Cochise was told of this development, and he was saddened. It had been bad enough when they were at peace with the whites, but now they would indeed be hunted down like the slinking coyotes of the hills. He yearned for Naretena and his wise, calm reasoning. *Naretena!* If only he, Cochise, had been wise enough to know what to do to that *nan-tan* Bascom! If only the Voice had warned him!

The Voice spoke to him very often now. His conscience ate at his insides. *The dead! The dead men of my people. Gone, walking now in the spirit world, they seem to be crying out to me. . . . Soon I shall be walking with them.*

"Mangas Coloradas has been killed," a breathless scout reported a year or so after the Apache Pass debacle.

"Where?" Cochise cried out. "How? Who did that thing?"

"White soldiers. At the camp of the *nan-tan* Carleton at Tucson," the scout said. "Under a white flag they took him. They said that the officer wanted to make talk. When they got him inside the camp, they made him prisoner and bound his hands behind his back."

"Under the white flag!" Cochise exclaimed, thinking of Bascom and *his* white flag. "Go on."

"That night he went to sleep by the fire, with many guards around him. In the night one of them put his bayonet into the coals and when the blade was red-hot, he laid it across Mangas' feet. When Mangas leaped up, they shot him in the back. They said he was trying to escape. . . . Then . . . they scalped him. Scalped him and cut off his head. What they did with it we do not know."

"Look to yourself!"

Cochise remembered how confidently he had offered this advice to his son, Tahzay. Now the words came back to haunt him. How was he to look

to himself to master the situations which had developed. He had tried to befriend the Americans and he had been betrayed under a white flag. Now Mangas also had been betrayed.

Silently he turned away from the messenger and sought Tesalbinay, whose calm strength and woman's wisdom he had increasingly valued as he grew older.

She looked up from her weaving as he approached, but her smile faded when she saw the black look on his face.

"Evil sits on your shoulders, my husband," she said. "What thing has happened?"

"Mangas Coloradas is dead," he told her. "The American soldiers have killed him."

Tesalbinay did not ask how, where, when, or by whom. Her hands fell into her lap. She lowered her graying head and began a low wailing. Not until the first of her grief had been spent, did Cochise leave her side. Then he walked to the top of the nearest hill and stood facing the sunset with arms upraised. His soul was in turmoil. Fervently he asked the Great Father for guidance.

7

The Making of Peace

AFTER THE APACHE PASS defeat, the Chirichuas
began to turn away from Cochise, grumbling that
he was getting old and could no longer bring them
victories. In vain he tried to tell them that the old
ways of fighting were gone forever. Still thinking
that the howitzers of the Americans were wagons,
he said, "We must learn to shoot wagons at our
enemies, as they do."

He looked at his fine double-barreled shotgun

with the silver mountings. He had yearned for that gun, long ago. But already it was outmoded. There were rifles and pistols and the howitzers, those awkward pieces of equipment that could blast a hole in a hillside.

To the outside world Cochise became a legend. He was a man hunted continually — hated, feared, held guilty of both the crimes he had committed, and those other Indians committed. But this did not worry him when he was told of it. What worried him was that he could not think of a way to turn the situation to the advantage of his people.

The Civil War resulted in a great change in the Indian country of the great Southwest. The little forts had been abandoned and the troops had been withdrawn to serve elsewhere. Raids to the Mexican villages continued, but there were fewer clashes with the Americans.

Arizona was established as a separate territory on February 14, 1862, by the Confederate Congress. However, Union forces reoccupied Tucson later in the year, and Arizona Territory was organized by act of the United States Congress on February 24, 1863. At that time, Colonel James H. Carleton, of the First California Volunteers, was headquartered in Tucson, where many of the earliest dwellings erected by white men had fallen into ruin and had become the homes of horned toads and lizards.

Cochise had never seen Colonel Carleton, and he did not know Thomas Jonathan Jeffords, who had come to Tucson to supervise the delivery of mail from Tucson to Fort Bowie.

His scouts had told him about this young man. He knew the man had sandy whiskers, and that he was not only a dead shot, but also a very brave man. When he could not hire riders to carry the mail, he mounted a horse and carried it himself, getting into a skirmish with some of Cochise's band and nearly being killed in the fight.

When Cochise learned that Jeffords was learning the Apache language and was asking many of the half-breeds how to get in touch with the Chiricahua chief, Cochise became curious.

"Why does he want to see me?" he asked bitterly. "Does he want to be the one who kills me, and maybe cuts off my head? At least he is a brave man."

As he looked into the campfire that night and brooded about the plight of his people, he wondered whether "Sandy Whiskers" — Taglito in Indian language — was trustworthy as well as brave. With all his savage heart he wished for a white man with whom he could talk — one who spoke truth and only truth.

Was there such a man? And if there was, would he, Cochise, ever find him? He doubted whether such a white man lived. But if he could find one and make peace, it would not be too late for Tahzay and Nachise to live a good life.

Winter snows were again powdering the tips of the sentinel peaks around the Stronghold when one of the scouts reported signal fires in the valley.

"A white man and an Indian boy, Apache, have come from direction of Tucson. Boy made signal fires. Says man wants to talk to Cochise."

Later he said, "Now boy rides back. Man comes on, alone."

Cochise went to the lookout where he had so often waited and watched during his childhood. He watched the slow, steady advance of the lone visitor. The man seemed sure of himself. He seemed unafraid, though at any moment an arrow might end his life.

At the foot of the trail he made more signals. "I come as friend to see Cochise."

Cochise made no signals in return. Let the man walk into the trap if he was so foolhardy.

Finally, with the entire encampment watching and the Indian dogs going crazy at the first sniff of the unknown scent, the man rode through the cleft in the rocks. With eyes straight ahead and hands held high to show that he meant no harm, he rode to the center of the camp and dismounted.

An old woman hobbled out and took the reins of his horse. He unbuckled his cartridge belt and gave it to her, the pistol in its sheath. Then he gave her his hunting knife, and told her, in fairly good Apache, that she was to keep his things until he was ready to leave camp.

From behind a screen of brush Cochise had watched the man's every movement. Now, seeing that he was unarmed, his rifle still in its scabbard on the saddle, Cochise advanced slowly.

"Why are you here?" he asked abruptly, the wild glitter in his eyes.

"I am Tom Jeffords," the white man said, his blue eyes meeting the black ones squarely and without fear. "I have come to talk with you about many things."

Cochise stared at him. This man would talk? About what?

"I will listen," Cochise said, turning away.

Jeffords followed him into a wickiup and sat down, facing him. After a long interval of silence, Cochise signaled him to speak.

Jeffords leaned toward Cochise.

"Messengers ride back and forth across the desert carrying pieces of paper we call letters," he said. "These men do you no harm. What they carry in their saddlebags is of no value to your people. I have come to ask you to allow them to make these rides safely. To my knowledge you have killed twenty-one of them, and fourteen of them were men I had hired to work for me. I do not want my men to be killed so senselessly. There must be an end to this killing."

Cochise sat like a bronze statue, his gaze fixed on Jeffords' face. For another long interval there was silence, then Nalikadeya shyly entered with a pot of stew and set it between the men. Cochise dipped in with his fingers and drew out a piece of meat. Jeffords suddenly decided he was hungry, and he followed Cochise's example. The meat was venison, and very tender and good.

When they had finished eating, Cochise spoke, and it was with the fervent release of a man whose thoughts have too long been stifled.

"For twelve years I have been on the big warpath," he said. "When the boy *nan-tan* soldier killed my brother and my nephews, I vowed I would kill ten Americans for each of them. For every Chiricahua the soldiers of that man killed, and for each one killed at the Santa Rita mines, we have killed many times ten. We have been revenged. . . . I have longed for someone to talk to; a man with a good heart and a straight tongue. Are you that man, Taglito, Sandy Whiskers? If you are, we can be friends. Come. I will show you my camp."

The two walked; walked and talked. Cochise was hungry for news of the outside world. He had many questions, and because Jeffords did not understand all the Apache words, communication was slow.

For three days Jeffords stayed in the encampment. He came to admire Cochise and his problem. It touched him that a man of such fine qualities had wasted his talents in wanton killing, raiding, and plundering. When Cochise said, "Our time is passing. Soon we will be few, and our land will be ours no longer," Jeffords was deeply touched.

"You were right to think that you should learn the way of the white man," he told Cochise. "Your brother spoke truth when he told you that the white men would be as many as the raindrops. Your old life was almost perfect, but things change, and men must change with them. We cannot hold onto the past. It slips through one's fingers like dry sand."

Cochise looked up at the sheltering walls.

"These rock walls that close us in and protect us from the white men have seen many of us live and die. They, too, will crumble away some day. The water in our stream may dry up. But I will not be here to see it. It is my sons for whom I would have better conditions. . . . Tahzay! . . . Nachise! . . . Come."

The two boys came and touched fingers with Jeffords, but still were watchful and suspicious.

"They are fine young men," Jeffords told Cochise.

When, at the end of a memorable three days,
Jeffords prepared to leave the camp, Cochise felt a
real sense of loss.

"*Shee-kizzen,*" he said, using the Apache word
for brother, "you will always be safe among us. Do
not stay away too long. It is good to have someone
to talk with. You are a brave man and a truthful
one. We will never lie to each other."

"We will never lie to each other," Jeffords repeated, and this was a sacred promise.

The months that followed were among the hap-
piest that Cochise had ever known. Both he and
Jeffords knew that their own people looked at them
strangely, but neither allowed this to influence
them. And although many times Jeffords led soldiers against raiding Chiricahua war parties, this
did not affect their personal friendship.

Cochise had a sharp brain. He understood
much that other men of his tribe did not understand, and it was a joy for him to talk with a man
whose keenness matched his own.

"It is like living in two bodies to have a friend

you can trust," he told his sons after one of Jeffords'
visits. "When a man has a friend he can share his
thoughts and his visions with, he seems to grow
bigger."

When the Civil War ended, the flow of westward-bound emigrants began once more. In order
to protect these home-seekers, the War Department felt it imperative to find Cochise and Geronimo, called the "outlaw Apaches" because they
had refused, so far, to make treaties with the Government, and confine them to reservations.

Several other Apache bands had parleyed with
the white men and had been placed on reservations, under the supervision of agents, but Cochise
had consistently refused to parley with anyone,
and Geronimo was to be a source of annoyance to
the War Department for many years.

The thought of being confined to a reservation
was still enough to send Cochise into a towering
rage. He refused to meet with anyone except
Jeffords.

Jeffords was then acting as special agent for
Captain Farnsworth.

Into the Southwest with a commission to bring

Cochise to the bargaining table came General Oliver Otis Howard. Like Cochise's old friend, Silas St. John, General Howard had lost one arm.

He had first heard of Tom Jeffords at a dinner, when someone referred to Jeffords as an "Injun lover" who often visited Cochise. Howard quietly asked a few questions about Jeffords, discovering with mounting interest that here was a man who might help him discharge his duty.

"Do you mean that this Jeffords actually visits the Chiricahua chief in his camp?" Howard asked.

"Yes, sir, General. He's the only white man ever to bust into Cochise's Stronghold and come back alive," the man replied.

General Howard lost no time in getting acquainted with Jeffords.

"I want you to take me to Cochise," he told Jeffords.

Jeffords considered this request thoughtfully.

"The time is right," he decided. "I think Cochise is as eager as anyone for peace with the Americans. I'll take you to him on one condition: You'll do as I say. Go to him alone, without troops or guards."

General Howard insisted on taking his aide

with him, and Jeffords finally agreed that he might do so. He hired a son of Mangas Coloradas, named Chee, and another man, Ponce, who was a son-in-law of the old Warm Springs chief, to go with them. Two packers and a handyman completed the party.

As soon as they were within the range of Cochise and his roving scouts and warriors, Jeffords ordered signal fires arranged in a circle. Those signals told Cochise how many were in the party, and how many would go on up to the Stronghold. They carried the message that Taglito, whom Cochise now called "Brother," was the guide and that he had promised the General and his aide full protection.

This time the men were not allowed to enter the Stronghold until they had been checked by some of Cochise's men. At one overnight camping place they were sitting around the campfire when they heard a coyote call.

"Men coming," Chee said. "Stay still. I will answer."

He answered the ululating cry, then disappeared into the brush. When he returned, he was accompanied by a band of Cochise's warriors, with a man named Nolgee as their leader. This man knew Jeffords, but at first he was stiff and suspicious because of the Army uniforms worn by General Howard and his aide. To him, the Army spelled trouble.

Under the influence of coffee and tobacco, however, he relaxed and gave Jeffords the message he had been sent to deliver.

"Cochise will have *yoshti* with the General, maybe," he said. "He waits at Stronghold."

When they reached the foot of the trail that led up to the hidden valley, the others camped while Chee went on alone. After he had talked with Cochise, assuring him that Jeffords had come willingly and was not a prisoner of the Army men, he sent word to Jeffords to come up.

"Cochise will talk to the General," the message told them.

As it had been when Jeffords first visited the Stronghold, all activity in the camp was suspended as the visitors entered. The women shyly looked at the kind-faced, one-armed general, and from him to their proven friend, sandy-whiskered Tom Jeffords. The warriors stood with folded arms, apprehensive and wondering if this, truly, might mean the end of their long campaign against the Americans, both soldiers and civilians. Even the naked babies stopped playing in the dirt and ran to cling to their mothers' skirts.

Tall, impressive, wearing his best fringed deerskins, his long leggings, his jewelry, and a bright shirt with the tail hanging out, Cochise came to greet the visitors.

"If the white men want peace, I am ready," he told Jeffords in Apache, and Jeffords relayed the welcome message to the General.

"But, before we talk," Cochise went on, "we must feast and dance and blow the cloud together."

It was an evening of great animation and good feeling. The drums throbbed; the women sang; the warriors whooped; the crown dancers in their high headdresses and fringed kilts performed their exuberant athletic dance, and the black-masked one made the bull-roarer bellow.

The next day there was much smoking, thinking, and talking. Cochise was not to be hurried. On every point he consulted with his men, the group including his sons, who would one day follow him as leaders of the Chiricahuas. It was eight days be-

fore the sub-chiefs unanimously agreed to the
treaty that Cochise proposed, and then only on
condition that Tom Jeffords be appointed their
agent. Above all white men, the Apaches trusted
Sandy Whiskers.

At first Jeffords was reluctant to take the re-
sponsibility of the agency of a reservation. He

sorrowed at the thought of his friends having to yield their wonderful free life to the demands of a changing world. Besides, this was not the normal manner of concluding a treaty, with the Indians dictating their own terms.

Howard, it became plain, was most sympathetic to the cause of the Apaches. He agreed that their terms could be met if Jeffords would agree, and when it became apparent that much depended on him, Jeffords consented.

Under the terms of the treaty no one, either civilian or soldier, could come onto the reservation without first gaining Jeffords' consent.

Cochise and his people were the only Apache band that went voluntarily onto the reservation established for them. For the next two years Cochise religiously kept the promises which he had made to General Howard. He and Jeffords remained the best of friends.

But the once strong chief of the Chiricahuas was getting old. His health was failing rapidly. The medicine men worked, but they could not restore the chief's health.

There came a day when Cochise called for his two sons.

"I am pleased with you," he told them when they came to his wickiup and knelt beside him. "When we were on the warpath, you were always at my side. You were brave warriors. Now I am about to leave you. I do not know where I am going. Maybe I will go to meet Naretena and Mangas Coloradas, my brothers. Maybe I will see my mother and my father who have walked the spirit path before me. I do not know.

"Tahzay, you will be head chief of all the Chiricahuas when I am gone. You will keep the peace treaty I have made with the *nan-tan* Howard. Nachise will help you."

"It is well," the young men agreed. "We will do as you have told us."

"I think we will meet again, somewhere, sometime, maybe," the dying chief said, closing his eyes.

Those who sat with him watched closely, knowing that the end was near. But after a moment, he opened his eyes.

"I would like to see Grandfather Sun once more," he murmured weakly. "I wish to watch him climb the mountain in the east . . ."

The boys understood. They brought a litter and lifted Cochise gently onto it, then took him up the hill. Members of his family followed silently.

The sun climbed up slowly in spreading radiance. It was shining on the craggy face of the man when his soul took flight.

All the shadows had fled.

Some Indian Terms

BULL-ROARER — A flat board at the end of a thong, which makes a roaring sound when twirled rapidly through the air.

CARRETA — A Spanish cart, which in primitive days had wooden wheels.

CRADLEBOARD — A carrying board onto which the Indian baby is laced with thongs. The cradleboard is usually covered with a wicker arch to shield the child's eyes from the sun.

KEENING — Wailing for the dead.

MESQUITE — A shrub of the Southwest (U.S.), the screw bean.

MOCCASIN GAME — An Apache "winter game."

NAN-TAN — An Apache word, meaning "leader."

PALOVERDE — A desert tree.

PINOLE — A meal ground from seeds, usually corn, in the Southwest.

POULTS — Young turkeys.

ROADRUNNER — A bird of the cuckoo family.

SAGUARO — A desert tree cactus, sometimes growing as tall as fifty feet.

SHEE-KIZZEN — The Apache word for "brother."

TISWIN — An intoxicating drink made from the desert plant mescal.

WICKIUP — An Apache lodge made of poles and brush.

YOSHTI — An Apache word meaning "the big smoke," indulged in by Apache men when in council.

Acknowledgment

Help received from the following historical records and other publications listed is hereby gratefully acknowledged by the author:

ARNOLD, ELLIOTT. *Blood Brother.* New York: Duell, Sloan & Pearce, 1950.

CLUM, WOODWORTH. *Apache Agent, The Story of John Philip Clum.* Boston: Houghton, Mifflin Company, 1936.

EGGAN, FRED, Editor. *Social Anthropology of North American Indian Tribes* (Morris E. Opler Essay on Apache Life Ways). Chicago: University of Chicago Press, 1937.

FARISH, THOMAS EDWIN. *History of Arizona.* San Francisco: The Filmer Brothers Electrotype Company (Vol. II).

LaFARGE, OLIVER. *A Pictorial History of the American Indians.* New York: Crown Publishers, Inc., 1950.

LOCKWOOD, FRANK C. *The Apache Indians.* New York: The Macmillan Company, 1938.

POSTON, CHARLES DIBRELL. *Apache-land.* San Francisco: A. L. Bancroft & Co., Printers, 1878.

WELLMAN, PAUL I., *Death in the Desert.* New York: The Macmillan Company, 1935.

WYLLYS, RUFUS K. *Arizona, The History of a Frontier State.* Phoenix, Arizona: Hobson & Herr, 1950.

About the Author

Vada Carlson's deep love and knowledge of Indian cultures stem from having lived near Indian reservations most of her life—in Nebraska near the Sioux during her early childhood, later in Wyoming just across the river from the Shoshone and Arapahoe tribes, and now in Arizona close to the Navahos, the Hopi, and the Apaches. Mrs. Carlson has received a number of awards and honors for her writings including the "Woman of Achievement" award from the National Federation of Press Women. She and her husband make their home in Winslow, Arizona.

About the Artist

William Orr's interest in American Indians had its roots in his living near the Gela River Apache Reservation in Arizona. His extensive research to portray the characters in the story of Cochise took him to the Library of Congress and to the Smithsonian Institute in order to authenticate his portrayals. When he could not obtain daguerrotypes of a particular Indian, he made an exhaustive study of pictures of that man's relatives in order to create as true a likeness as possible. Bill Orr makes his home in Florida.